12/98

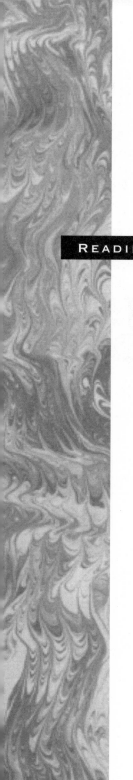

READINGS ON

# ANIMAL FARM

## Other titles in the Greenhaven Press Literary Companion Series:

### AMERICAN AUTHORS

Maya Angelou
Stephen Crane
Emily Dickinson
William Faulkner
F. Scott Fitzgerald
Nathaniel Hawthorne
Ernest Hemingway
Herman Melville
Arthur Miller
Eugene O'Neill
Edgar Allan Poe
John Steinbeck
Mark Twain

### BRITISH AUTHORS

Jane Austen
Joseph Conrad
Charles Dickens

### WORLD AUTHORS

Fyodor Dostoyevsky
Homer
Sophocles

### AMERICAN LITERATURE

The Great Gatsby
Of Mice and Men
The Scarlet Letter

### BRITISH LITERATURE

The Canterbury Tales
Lord of the Flies
Romeo and Juliet
Shakespeare: The Comedies
Shakespeare: The Sonnets
Shakespeare: The Tragedies
A Tale of Two Cities

### WORLD LITERATURE

The Diary of a Young Girl

THE GREENHAVEN PRESS
*Literary Companion*
TO BRITISH LITERATURE

READINGS ON

# ANIMAL FARM

David Bender, *Publisher*
Bruno Leone, *Executive Editor*
Brenda Stalcup, *Managing Editor*
Bonnie Szumski, *Series Editor*
Terry O'Neill, *Book Editor*

Greenhaven Press, San Diego, CA

Every effort has been made to trace the owners of copyrighted material. The articles in this volume may have been edited for content, length, and/or reading level. The titles have been changed to enhance the editorial purpose of the Opposing Viewpoints® concept. Those interested in locating the original source will find the complete citation on the first page of each article.

Library of Congress Cataloging-in-Publication Data

Readings on Animal farm / Terry O'Neill, book editor.
  p.    cm. — (Greenhaven Press literary
companion to British literature)
  Includes bibliographical references and index.
  ISBN 1-56510-651-2 (lib. bdg. : alk. paper). —
ISBN 1-56510-650-4 (pbk. : alk. paper)
  1. Orwell, George, 1903–1950. Animal farm. 2. Orwell,
George, 1903–1950—Political and social views. 3. Politics
and literature—Great Britain—History—20th century.
4. Political fiction, English—History and criticism.
5. Satire, English—History and criticism. 6. Fables,
English—History and criticism. 7. Social problems in
literature. 8. Animals in literature. I. O'Neill, Terry,
1944–  . II. Series.
PR6029.R8A766   1998
823'.912—dc21                                           97-22683
                                                            CIP

Cover photo: AKG Photo

Copyright ©1998 by Greenhaven Press, Inc.
PO Box 289009
San Diego, CA 92198-9009
Printed in the U.S.A.

*❝What I have most
wanted to do . . . is to
make political writing
into an art.❞*

—*George Orwell, "Why I Write"*

# CONTENTS

# FOREWORD

*"'Tis the good reader that
makes the good book."*

Ralph Waldo Emerson

The story's bare facts are simple: The captain, an old and scarred seafarer, walks with a peg leg made of whale ivory. He relentlessly drives his crew to hunt the world's oceans for the great white whale that crippled him. After a long search, the ship encounters the whale and a fierce battle ensues. Finally the captain drives his harpoon into the whale, but the harpoon line catches the captain about the neck and drags him to his death.

A simple story, a straightforward plot—yet, since the 1851 publication of Herman Melville's *Moby-Dick*, readers and critics have found many meanings in the struggle between Captain Ahab and the whale. To some, the novel is a cautionary tale that depicts how Ahab's obsession with revenge leads to his insanity and death. Others believe that the whale represents the unknowable secrets of the universe and that Ahab is a tragic hero who dares to challenge fate by attempting to discover this knowledge. Perhaps Melville intended Ahab as a criticism of Americans' tendency to become involved in well-intentioned but irrational causes. Or did Melville model Ahab after himself, letting his fictional character express his anger at what he perceived as a cruel and distant god?

Although literary critics disagree over the meaning of *Moby-Dick*, readers do not need to choose one particular interpretation in order to gain an understanding of Melville's novel. Instead, by examining various analyses, they can gain

numerous insights into the issues that lie under the surface
of the basic plot. Studying the writings of literary critics can
also aid readers in making their own assessments of *Moby-
Dick* and other literary works and in developing analytical
thinking skills.

The Greenhaven Literary Companion Series was created
with these goals in mind. Designed for young adults, this
unique anthology series provides an engaging and comprehensive introduction to literary analysis and criticism. The
essays included in the Literary Companion Series are chosen for their accessibility to a young adult audience and are
expertly edited in consideration of both the reading and
comprehension levels of this audience. In addition, each
essay is introduced by a concise summation that presents
the contributing writer's main themes and insights. Every
anthology in the Literary Companion Series contains a varied selection of critical essays that cover a wide time span
and express diverse views. Wherever possible, primary
sources are represented through excerpts from authors'
notebooks, letters, and journals and through contemporary
criticism.

Each title in the Literary Companion Series pays careful
consideration to the historical context of the particular author or literary work. In-depth biographies and detailed
chronologies reveal important aspects of authors' lives and
emphasize the historical events and social milieu that influenced their writings. To facilitate further research, every anthology includes primary and secondary source bibliogra-
phies of articles and/or books selected for their suitability
for young adults. These engaging features make the Greenhaven Literary Companion Series ideal for introducing students to literary analysis in the classroom or as a library re-
source for young adults researching the world's great
authors and literature.

Exceptional in its focus on young adults, the Greenhaven
Literary Companion Series strives to present literary criticism in a compelling and accessible format. Every title in the
series is intended to spark readers' interest in leading American and world authors, to help them broaden their understanding of literature, and to encourage them to formulate
their own analyses of the literary works that they read. It is
the editors' hope that young adult readers will find these an-
thologies to be true companions in their study of literature.

# INTRODUCTION

George Orwell's *Animal Farm* is more than a half century old and is still being read and discussed in schools, colleges, and homes. At first glance it is a simple little tale—Orwell himself called it "a fairy-tale"—so what makes this novel an enduring work worthy of classroom study? The essays in this collection from the Greenhaven Literary Companion Series address that question.

*Animal Farm* has been controversial since its inception. Orwell, distressed by events in Russia between the world wars, was determined to write a work that would speak to all people and make them realize the way Russian Communists had betrayed the socialist ideal as set out in Karl Marx and Friedrich Engels's famous work *The Communist Manifesto* (1848). Orwell wanted to examine not only the Russian Revolution, but the cause of what he believed was its failure. *Animal Farm*, completed in 1944, was his answer. He felt it was important to publish it at a time when Great Britain and the United States were allied with Russia in trying to defeat Adolf Hitler and Nazi Germany. He wanted the free world not to be deluded about the nature of this ally. However, he had difficulty finding a publisher (four rejected the manuscript) for this politically sensitive book, and by the time it appeared (August 1945 in Britain, 1946 in the United States), the war in Europe was over and the former Allies were squaring off over the devastated continent. Despite the Allies' rapid falling out, *Animal Farm*'s publication was greeted with both delight and horror. Many people were offended and concerned by its implied but obvious criticism of Britain's Russian ally. Others were charmed by its fairy-tale quality. Few readers were unaffected by its portrayal of the animals who seek to overthrow their tyrannical master, Farmer Jones, but who end up not in an animal Eden but in a society as tyrannical as the one they overthrew.

*Animal Farm* was Orwell's first widely successful novel.

It and *1984* stand as his most lasting works. Both deal with issues of freedom and tyranny. These were his last novels. Many people wonder what direction his writing, seemingly at its most powerful in these two novels, would have gone had he not died at an early age.

This volume is divided into three parts. The first section shows some of the reactions to the novel when it first came out—the early reviews. The other two parts each contain a range of essays that cover the fifty-some years since the book was first published. The essays in part two debate the novel's literary merits; part three demonstrates the debate over the novel's social and political meaning. The careful reader will also see how the views have been affected by the times in which they were written.

The contributors to this collection are literary critics, academics, and colleagues of Orwell. Their essays have been chosen for ease of understanding and the strength of their comments on *Animal Farm.*

Additional features of this Literary Companion that will aid the reader's understanding include brief exploratory introductions to each article; subheads; and brief quotations from other sources inserted into some of the featured articles. A biographical introduction to George Orwell clarifies the experiences and political philosophy that led Orwell to write *Animal Farm.* A detailed chronology puts events in Orwell's life in the context of events of the time in which he lived. A bibliography suggests further works for the reader who wants to know more about Orwell, his world, and *Animal Farm.*

# GEORGE ORWELL: A LIFE

"I had no money, I was weak, I was ugly, I was unpopular, I had a chronic cough, I was cowardly, I smelt. . . . The conviction that it *was not possible* for me to be a success went deep enough to influence my life."

The adult George Orwell, a novelist known round the world, wrote these self-deprecating remarks in an essay reflecting on his days as a student at St. Cyprian's, a costly private school at which he had been a scholarship student. Was his self-disparagement true? A number of accounts say that Orwell exaggerated. His childhood friend, Jacintha Buddicom, wrote in her memoir, *Eric and Us,* of the fun she and her siblings had with Orwell when he was a boy. The children hunted and fished, played games, and tried adventurous experiments. (One time Orwell and Jacintha's brother, Prosper, tried to build a whiskey still on the Buddicoms' kitchen stove. When they turned on the heat, it exploded. This incident, which shortly followed their experiment using the stove to cook a hedgehog in a mud coffin, inspired the Buddicom family cook to quit.)

Many of the bitter and sad things Orwell wrote about his childhood were viewed from the perspective of his later years, when his acute ill health may have influenced his views. Or perhaps Tom Hopkinson is right. Hopkinson, author of the short critical biography *George Orwell,* written for the British Council and the National Book League in 1953, explains Orwell as "a somewhat irritable man whose writings tended to over-emphasize the gloomy aspects of every subject and experience he treated." Much of Orwell's life was a struggle—a struggle to overcome ill health and his own sensitivity, to go his own way rather than the way his parents and his political colleagues expected of him, and to achieve a self-supporting career as a writer. And even during his most vital years, when he traveled England and France investigating the living conditions of the poor, participated in the Spanish Civil War, married, and worked within a lively literary crowd, the struggle for a living wage, health, and independence never left him.

One friend from the years of his early adulthood, Ruth Pitter, described him this way: "His nature was divided. There was something like a high wall right across the middle of it. A high wall with flowers and fruit and running water on one side, and the desert on the other." He loved life, but he despaired from its struggles.

## EARLY YEARS

Although George Orwell is a British writer, he was born in India—and his name was not George Orwell. His father, Richard Blair, was one of the thousands of British civil servants who served their country in foreign lands. In 1903, when Orwell was born Eric Blair, England was still a strong colonial power. The small island nation had spent much of the past centuries conquering foreign lands, including the Indian subcontinent. As in most of its colonies, a large population of English nationals lived in India and administered its government. Richard Blair was a minor official involved in monitoring the opium trade, at that time a legal and lucrative business for England, which sold the opium to China.

Richard Blair had married at the late age of thirty-nine. His wife, the former Ida Limouzin, was twenty-one at the time. She was the daughter of an English mother and a French father, and she had spent most of her life up to that time in Burma, where her father ran a teakwood business. Ida was a lively, independent, and well-read woman, while all reports suggest that Richard was rather dull and conventional. Little Eric was the family's second child. His older sister, Marjorie, had been born five years earlier.

When Eric was only a year old, his mother took the two children and moved to England. Richard stayed in India until his retirement in 1912, with only one visit back to England—for three months in 1907—during which Eric's younger sister, Avril, was conceived. The family's living arrangement was not uncommon for British civil servants of the time; children of English parents posted in foreign lands were often returned to England when it was time for them to go to school. Nevertheless, Richard Blair's absence during much of Eric's childhood contributed to the distance that remained between the two men during their entire lives. Years after he had reached adulthood, Orwell wrote,

Looking back on my own childhood, after the infant years were over, I do not believe that I ever felt love for any mature person, except my mother, and even her I did not trust, in the sense that shyness made me conceal most of my real feelings from her. . . . I merely disliked my father, whom I had barely seen before I was eight and who appeared to me simply as a gruff-voiced elderly man forever saying "Don't."

## SCHOOL DAYS

Orwell remembered pleasantly his early school days in a small private school near his home. But when he turned eight, his mother decided that it was time for him to go away to boarding school, another common practice among middle-class families of the time. He was sent to St. Cyprian's, sixty miles south of London, a school known for getting its students into the prestigious prep school Eton. From there a good student would certainly be accepted at Cambridge, Oxford, or another distinguished university.

Little Eric was not ready to go away to school. He was homesick and shy, and his memoir of those school days, an essay called "Such, Such Were the Joys," published two years after his death, told of beatings and abuse by other students and, more significantly, by the mercurial, domi-nating schoolmistress and her husband. Many former St. Cyprians asserted that Orwell's essay was inaccurate and exaggerated, but Orwell clearly hated the place and felt it had done poorly by him. Even so, he did well in his studies there (he also had his first poem published during this time—a patriotic piece called "Awake Young Men of En-gland"), and he did indeed win a scholarship to Eton when he was thirteen.

His stay at Eton was more comfortable but not particu-larly distinguished academically. He later wrote, "I did no work there and learned very little," although he did appreci-ate the school. In a 1948 essay, "For Ever Eton," he praised the school's "tolerant and civilized atmosphere which gives each boy a fair chance of developing his individuality," a quality highly valued by Orwell. Unfortunately, his perfor-mance at Eton did not earn him a university scholarship, and his father, who was now retired and supporting the fam-ily on his pension, refused to pay for him to go to college. His father hoped that Eric would go into civil service as he him-self had done. He also hoped the young man would give up his silly and impractical notions of becoming a writer.

## THE EXPERIENCE OF IMPERIALISM

Disappointed that he would not be able to go to university, Eric joined the colonial police service in 1922 and was sent to Burma for the next five years. Here his real education in the nature of colonialism took place. This was probably where he consciously awakened to the injustice inherent in societies built on strong class distinctions and the power of one class over another. Eric and other British officials had much more power in this foreign land than did its natives. And Burmese society itself comprised strongly delineated social classes.

Though Orwell participated in the disparities of the colonial empire (he later wrote, "When you have a lot of servants, you soon get into lazy habits, and I habitually allowed myself, for instance, to be dressed and undressed by my Burmese boy"), Eric learned lessons here that he was to call upon time and again in his nonfiction and novels, including *Animal Farm.* Critic David Wykes commented that his time in Burma "taught Orwell about himself, gave him the subjects for a full-length novel [*Burmese Days*] and two of his most impressive essays ['Shooting an Elephant' and 'A Hanging'], and shaped one of the permanent strands of his personal belief." Eric came to see imperialism as a greed-motivated political system, with one power (in this case, his own country) exploiting weaker people in order to gain wealth.

During the time Eric was in Burma, a strong native nationalist movement was rebelling against British authority. The political tensions intensified class and racial distinctions. In his 1934 novel *Burmese Days*, one of his characters says bitterly of himself:

> In the end the secrecy of your revolt poisons you like a secret disease.... Year after year you sit in Kipling-haunted little Clubs, ... listening and eagerly agreeing while Colonel Bodger develops his theory that these bloody Nationalists should be boiled in oil. You hear your Oriental friends called "greasy little babus," and you admit, dutifully, that they *are* greasy little babus. You see louts fresh from school kicking greyhaired servants. The time comes when you burn with hatred of your own countrymen, when you long for a native rising to drown their Empire in blood.

In his 1937 book *The Road to Wigan Pier*, an account of the lives of British coal miners, he wrote, "Every Anglo-Saxon [in a British colony] is haunted by a sense of guilt.... All over India there are Englishmen who secretly loathe the system of which they are a part."

## TRAMPING

Home on leave after five years, Eric decided not to return to Burma. He left the police and, in an effort to understand the people he had helped repress during the previous five years, he began what he called tramping—mingling with the poorest classes of people in England. His political awareness aroused, as well as his eagerness to write, he informed his parents that he was going to become a writer and that he was going to make his own way, not burdening them while he tried to build a career.

Perhaps inspired in part by Jack London, the American writer who had lived among London's poor near the beginning of the twentieth century and written about them in his book *The People of the Abyss*, Orwell went to London. There he found an inexpensive boarding house in a respectable part of the city, but he spent most of his days and some of his nights in London's impoverished and crime-ridden East End. He dressed shabbily and mingled with the poor people of the district. In *The Road to Wigan Pier*, Orwell wrote that he had rejected "every form of man's dominion over man," and now he wanted "to get right down among the oppressed, to be one of them and on their side against their tyrants."

He lived similarly in Paris in 1928–29, where he suffered one of many bouts with serious lung-related illness. With a severe case of pneumonia, he experienced the health care received by France's poor at the time. His hospital stay later resulted in a horrific essay, "How the Poor Die." His experiences among the poor also resulted, four years later, in his first published book, *Down and Out in Paris and London* (1933), and his first use of the pseudonym George Orwell.

Blair had wanted a pseudonym, suggests biographer Michael Shelden, because of his insecurities and his belief that he was not capable of achieving success. If the book did not succeed, he would not have to feel embarrassed among people who knew him only as Eric Blair. His publisher, Victor Gollancz, originally wanted to use "X" as Blair's pseudonym, so Blair came up with a list of seven names, of which "George Orwell" was his own favorite. Gollancz agreed. The book received good reviews and was a modest sales success, so Blair decided to stick with the pseudonym. Although many of his old friends still called him Eric Blair, in the writing world he was known as George Orwell after 1934.

By 1930 Eric had begun to see his book reviews and articles fairly frequently accepted by the magazine *Adelphi.* This was his entree to the writing world. Although it took years before he earned a real living at it, he was now in contact with a strong network of other writers and publishers, and he began to find work writing literary and political pieces. Over the next few years, he also tutored private students, taught school, and worked in a bookstore to supplement his meager writing income. At the end of 1933, he suffered another bout of pneumonia and was forced to quit teaching. He moved back to his parents' home to convalesce and began work on his second work of fiction, *A Clergyman's Daughter.* His health returned quickly, and he moved back to London in October 1934. Six months later, he met Eileen Maud O'Shaughnessy, the woman who would become his wife in 1936.

## EILEEN

Eileen O'Shaughnessy was a graduate student working on a degree in educational psychology when she and Orwell met. She lived with her brother, Laurence, a surgeon and tuberculosis specialist, and his wife. A friend described Eileen as "a very happy person . . . [with] a vivid personality. . . . She was untiring in her efforts to help people." Eileen and Orwell were immediately attracted to each other, and the day after they met, Orwell remarked to a friend that she was "the sort of girl I'd like to marry." Eileen was independent, intelligent, had a good sense of humor, and was not reluctant to contradict Orwell, who had a tendency to exaggerate and make wild generalizations.

In January 1936, Orwell went on the road again, this time to northern England, where he was to research the lives of the poor and unemployed in this coal-mining area. He spent about two months living in a squalid boardinghouse and talking with the people there. The people he met either had no jobs or worked at low-paying, exceedingly dangerous mine positions. Orwell wrote about their lives in *The Road to Wigan Pier.* His experiences with the miners reinforced his political views:

> The people who have got to act together are all those who cringe to the boss and all those who shudder when they think of the rent. This means that the small holder [farmer] has got to ally himself with the factory-hand, the typist with the coal miner, the schoolmaster with the garage mechanic.

He was by now committed to many of the views professed by

socialists—including the belief that people needed to work together and to share both the responsibilities and rewards of their work. Their lives would improve if they did this, he believed, but would only deteriorate further if they did no more than kowtow to those who held spurious power over them.

Orwell and Eileen O'Shaughnessy married in June of that year. They lived in a rented seventeenth-century cottage in the tiny rural community of Hertfordshire, where they wrote, gardened, raised a few animals, and operated a small store from their living room. In fact, their home was called The Stores. They lived a pleasant, quiet life for several months, despite the war that was looming in Spain. But by December, Orwell knew he had to go to Spain to be part of the fight.

## SPAIN

General Francisco Franco had led a revolt against Spain's elected government and was attempting to gain dictatorial powers. The government, a Republican coalition of workers and the middle class called the Popular Front, had formed armed militias, which many people from other countries were joining in their fight against Franco's fascism. The militias represented several different political groups, professing mostly anarchist or communist views. During most of his six months there, Orwell worked and fought with POUM (*Partido Obrero de Unificación Marxista*, or Workers' Party of Marxist Unification), an anarchist group that ultimately wanted to see an end to centralized government, in favor of individuals and communities governing themselves. But for the duration of this struggle they were willing to fight beside Communists (who were closely aligned with the Soviet Union, at this time dominated by the dictator Joseph Stalin), and beside the bourgeoisie or business class, in order to defeat the greater evil of fascism. For a time, Orwell left POUM and joined the Communists, but he was disillusioned by their connection to the dictator Stalin. Stalin was beginning his great purge, in which he was responsible for the deaths of millions of Russians who he believed were not loyal to his absolute rule.

Robert Edwards, a war colleague, gave this colorful description of Orwell in Spain:

> He came striding towards me—all 6 foot 3 of him—dressed in a grotesque mixture of clothing—corduroy riding breeches, khaki puttees and huge boots caked with mud, a yellow

pigskin jerkin, a chocolate-coloured balaclava helmet with a
knitted khaki scarf of immeasurable length wrapped round
and round his neck and face up to his ears, an old-fashioned
German rifle over his shoulder and two hand-grenades hanging from his belt. Running to keep pace, one on each side of
him, similarly equipped, were two small youths of the militia,
whilst farther behind was a shaggy mongrel dog with the letters POUM painted on its side.

Orwell was a soldier and a trainer of new recruits. He frequently despaired of the undisciplined, untrained, and
poorly equipped men and boys who made up the Spanish
militias. He spent hour after hour training them, trying to
make them into efficient soldiers. And, says Roberts, they
worshiped him for it. Eileen also went to Spain in early 1936
and worked for the International Labor Party in Barcelona.

In May, Orwell was hit in the throat by an enemy bullet,
which narrowly missed his carotid artery. While he was
convalescing, he and Eileen were forced to flee Spain sur-
reptitiously, for amid unstable alliances, political infighting
had led the government to accuse them and many others involved in POUM of treason. With two friends, they managed
to get safely to France by train, and from there they returned
to England.

In spite of his forced departure, Orwell's experience in
Spain reinforced his political views and resulted in his 1939
book *Homage to Catalonia.* In it he wrote, "I have seen wonderful things and at last really believe in Socialism." Critic
David Wykes says his experience in Spain was "the single
greatest formative influence" on his political ideas, and that
"Revolutionary Barcelona was the city of his dreams. . . .
What he first saw was how a truly egalitarian society would
work." Orwell himself wrote:

> It was the first time that I had ever been in a town where the
> working class was in the saddle. . . . Above all, there was a be-
> lief in the revolution and the future, a feeling of having sud-
> denly emerged into an era of equality and freedom. Human
> beings were trying to behave as human beings and not as
> cogs in the capitalist machine.

And in a later piece written for a publication called *Time
and Tide,* he wrote:

> For several months large blocks of people believed that all
> men are equal and were able to act on their belief. The result
> was a feeling of liberation and hope. . . . No one who was in
> Spain during the months when people still believed in the
> revolution will ever forget that strange and moving experi-

ence. It has left something behind that no dictatorship, not even Franco's, will be able to efface.

As with other of his books, Orwell had some difficulty getting *Homage to Catalonia* published. Gollancz had given the unknown Eric Blair his first break and had published several of his previous books, but was always sensitive to possible libel problems. Minimizing the risk had required significant rewriting in some of the books. Victor Gollancz was a dedicated Communist, and *Homage to Catalonia*, while supportive of leftist ideals in general, was critical of communism. Gollancz, who held "right of first refusal" for the next several Orwell manuscripts, refused the book. Another publisher, however, gladly took it. That publisher, Secker and Warburg, ultimately published all of Orwell's later books.

In February 1938, Orwell suffered another terrible attack of ill health, coughing and spitting up blood. His weight was down to 159 pounds. Chest X rays showed deep shadows. All his symptoms pointed to tuberculosis, but medical tests did not at first confirm that diagnosis. Nevertheless, Orwell spent almost six months in a sanatorium, followed by six months in Marrakesh, Morocco. By the time he and Eileen returned to their cottage in England, Orwell's father was dying from intestinal cancer, and war with Hitler was imminent.

## WAR

When war did break out in September 1939, Orwell tried to enlist but was rejected because of his poor health. Eileen, however, did get a job with the Censorship Department in London. After several months alone in their cottage, Orwell, too, returned to London. He began writing book and film reviews and essays for *Time and Tide, Horizon,* and other magazines. He also joined the Home Guard, a civilian militia. Once again, he trained would-be soldiers, and he wrote inspirational and training materials for them.

During this time, Orwell noticed changes in his work habits. Where he formerly wrote several drafts of everything, now he was writing a single draft:

> Nowadays, when I write a review, I sit down at the typewriter and type it straight out. Till recently, indeed till six months ago, I never did this and would have said that I could not do it. Virtually all that I wrote was written at least twice, and my books as a whole three times—individual passages as many as five or ten times.

Despite evidence of careful attention to style, Orwell attributed this new facility to apathy toward his subject material.

His friend and colleague George Woodcock thought there was a different reason for Orwell's single-draft habit, a habit that was to stick with him throughout his magazine career. In a piece for *Commentary*, Woodcock wrote about the days he and Orwell worked together at *Tribune*, a magazine for which Orwell wrote a monthly column called "As I Please":

> I used to be surprised to watch Orwell writing an almost perfect "As I Please" piece straight on the typewriter, with no second version, but I think the reason for this facility as well as for his productivity under the circumstances of his life lay in the extent to which his writing was tied into his existence. . . . He liked to talk out his ideas in long monologues over cups of strong tea and hand-rolled cigarettes of black shag [tobacco], and not long afterward one would see the evening's talk appearing as an article, and not long after that the third stage would be reached when it was incorporated into a book.

Woodcock also wrote, "His writing seemed effortless, but it was so only because of the exacting discipline he imposed on structure and verbal texture alike." Orwell had many critics, of both his writing style and his ideas, but perhaps none was more harsh than Orwell himself.

The war years in London were tough ones. Orwell and his wife survived the blitz, when their apartment was sometimes literally falling down around them, and they survived rationing and attendant hardships. Perhaps most difficult for Orwell to deal with was the wartime censorship. When he had served in Burma, he had not felt free to speak his mind. Now he felt that way in London as well. A reflection of the impact of this repression can be seen in his final novel, *1984*, in which censorship, not only of words but of thoughts, is all-pervasive.

In 1941 Orwell accepted a position with the BBC, broadcasting programs to India, despite what has been described as his thin, high voice. One colleague, John Morris, who was head of the BBC Far Eastern Services during the time Orwell worked there, wrote of him in a 1950 issue of *Penguin New Writing*:

> He laughed often, but in repose his lined face suggested the grey asceticism of a medieval saint carved in stone and very weathered. . . . His most striking features were his luxuriant and unruly hair and the strange expression in his eyes, a combination of benevolence and fanaticism; it was as though he saw more (as indeed he did) than the ordinary mortal, and

pitied him for his lack of understanding. Although he wrote so well, he was a poor and halting speaker; even in private conversation he expressed himself badly and would often fumble for the right word. His weekly broadcast talks were beautifully written, but he delivered them in a dull and monotonous voice. I was often in the studio with him, and it was painful to hear such good material wasted: like many other brilliant writers, he never really understood the subtle differences between the written and the spoken word, or, if he did, could not be bothered with them.

Orwell's work entailed writing and presenting programs, usually with a literary or other intellectual theme, which were broadcast into India, still an integral part of the British Empire. The British were anxious to keep India psychologically attached to Britain, because they wanted to assure the loyalty and availability of India's army of more than 2 million men. All programs, of course, were first passed by the censors, and Orwell occasionally had a battle on his hands.

Orwell worked hard on the programs and was dismayed when a survey taken by an intelligence officer in India showed that few Indians listened to the programs, and that of all the regular speakers, Orwell was among the least popular. By the end of September 1943, Orwell had decided to move on.

## *Animal Farm*

He went back to focusing his efforts on magazine writing, and in November he became the literary editor of *Tribune*. In one of his "As I Please" columns, Orwell described the publication as "the only existing weekly paper that makes a genuine effort to be both progressive and humane—that is, to combine a radical Socialist policy with a respect for freedom of speech and a civilized attitude towards literature and the arts."

It was also during this time that he began work on *Animal Farm*, the short novel that was to become his first bestselling novel both in Britain and the United States. Biographer Michael Shelden says that

> the idea for the book had been in the back of his mind since his return from Spain. Having barely escaped from the long reach of Stalin's agents, he began to reflect on how a genuine revolutionary movement in Spain could have allowed itself to come so completely under the control of a dictator living thousands of miles away.

Orwell felt that the Spanish Communists, as well as many left-wing thinkers in Britain and other countries, had been swayed by the "Soviet myth"—the idea that the Russian Revolution had glorified the common people and placed them in a "worker's paradise." And, writes Shelden, "What better way to fight that myth than to create a mythical story of animals whose successful revolt against tyranny degenerates into a greedy struggle for power?"

Orwell had much experience with animals during his lifetime, from the ones raised on the land of his childhood friends, to the donkeys of Burma, to the chickens and goats he and Eileen had raised at their cottage. He models some of the animal behavior in his book on these real animals, although, clearly, his *Animal Farm* creatures have more human than animal traits. Apparently, Orwell and Eileen discussed every detail of this book during its writing, with her reading and commenting and then enthusiastically telling her work colleagues about Orwell's latest novel.

Orwell knew that because of Gollancz's communist sympathies, he would not publish *Animal Farm*. Yet he was obligated to offer him the book first. When Gollancz did indeed turn it down, Orwell offered it to three other publishers before the fourth, Secker and Warburg, accepted it. Because of the war and the Soviet Union's alliance with Britain, the anti-Stalin feelings raised by Stalin's purges had been muted, and no publisher wanted to risk offending Stalin or his supporters. Secker and Warburg, however, agreed with Orwell that this was an important book. Even so, none of them realized just how big an impact the novel would have. It sold more than 25,000 copies in Britain between 1945 and 1950 and nearly 600,000 in the United States between 1946 and 1950 (thanks largely to its being chosen as a Book-of-the-Month Club selection)—unheard-of figures for Orwell, whose best books typically sold only a few thousand copies.

## FAMILY MAN

Two other major events in Orwell's life occurred while he was writing *Animal Farm*: In March 1943, his mother died, and just over a year later he and Eileen adopted a child, Richard Horatio Blair. Orwell had wanted a child for some time, and his need became stronger after his mother's death. He and Eileen were unable to bear a child together, so with the help of Eileen's sister, a physician, they found a baby. The couple was ecstatic.

In March 1945, World War II was winding down, and because of his health, Orwell had seen no action beyond drilling with the Home Guard and enduring the very real dangers of the London blitz. He managed to get commissioned to go to France to do some end-of-the-war reporting. While there, he received a message from Eileen, whose health had badly declined during the stressful war years. She wrote that she needed an operation, but that she was concerned about the cost. Orwell cabled back to her to go ahead. And the next word he received—the following day—was that she had died from complications of anesthesia. Orwell was stunned. In poor health once again himself, he managed to get home in time for her funeral. Suddenly Orwell was a widower, and a single parent.

Orwell made temporary arrangements for Richard and returned to Europe to continue his reporting. "I felt so upset at home," he wrote to a friend, "I thought I would rather be on the move for a bit." But by June, he was back home again and had found a housekeeper and nanny, Susan Watson. She took care of baby Richard while Orwell went back to his writing routine. Watson said that he would work all morning, then go out to lunch with friends, work all afternoon, and take another break for high tea, then go back to work, often until late into the night. In the year following Eileen's death, reports Michael Shelden, Orwell wrote more than 130 articles and reviews, a formidable amount for any writer. This work kept him too busy to feel his grief and loneliness during the months following Eileen's death.

By spring of the following year, however, biographer Bernard Crick reports, Orwell's loneliness had come to the fore again. He missed married life, and in spite of Susan Watson's presence, he missed having a real mother for his son. Crick says that "within little more than a year of Eileen's death, he had proposed to at least four women, maybe more, and had been gently rejected." To one woman, he wrote a letter of proposal that included a rather eccentric approach: "What I am really asking you," he wrote, "is whether you would like to be the widow of a literary man." He said that his health was poor and that his books were beginning to show a nice profit, so after a relatively short time of marriage, the widow Orwell should have a comfortable income.

Although he did not acquire a wife during this time, he did meet the woman who would become his second wife only a few years later. Her name was Sonia Brownell. She worked for Cyril Connelly, an old friend of Orwell's, at Connelly's magazine *Horizon*, for which Orwell did some writing. Sonia was fifteen years younger than he, attractive, energetic, opinionated, and strong. Orwell found her fascinating, although they did not develop a relationship at this time.

## JURA

In the summer of 1946, Orwell, Richard, Susan Watson, and Watson's young daughter moved to the island of Jura in the Hebrides Islands off Scotland. A wealthy friend of Orwell's, David Astor, had told him of the place a couple of years before, and Orwell had been immediately intrigued. This seemed like a good time to go there; it would give him an escape from the many distractions of London, allow him to concentrate more fully on his writing, and expose his son to life in a wholesome rural area.

The house they lived in, a big, old place that had not been occupied since 1934, was called Barnhill. To get there one had to trek across seven or eight rugged miles or borrow a car or bicycle from one of the other few island residents. Mail was delivered only once a week, and there was only one telephone on the entire island. The house was big enough to give Orwell plenty of room for guests and playing children, as well as privacy and quiet to write. Psychologically, Orwell thrived there, although at least one invited guest did not share his enthusiasm for the place. Inez Holden recalled years later to a BBC interviewer, "George had a fantastically silly Robinson Crusoe mind."

Orwell's older sister, Marjorie, had died in the spring, and his younger sister, Avril, joined him on Jura. She seemed determined to take care of him and his household, and, according to Susan Watson, she essentially drove Watson out. Avril continued to take care of many of Orwell's needs for the rest of his life, and after his death she and her husband (she married an islander in 1951) adopted Richard and reared him as their own.

In August 1946, Orwell began work on his last novel, *1984*, which, along with *Animal Farm*, is one of his most enduring works. In October, with the novel barely begun, he and his entourage returned to London, where he spent an increasingly miserable winter. London was still subject to wartime rationing, and the entire city ran out of heating fuel before winter was over. In early April, Orwell returned to Barnhill, where he intended to stay.

Near the end of 1947, he completed the first draft of *1984*, and he checked into a sanatorium. He was coughing badly and spitting up blood, and he was, for the first time, officially diagnosed as having tuberculosis. David Astor anonymously helped pay for Orwell's treatment and secured the most advanced medical help available. Orwell spent seven months there, resting, recuperating, and trying to regain his health. When he finally went home to Jura in July, he immediately turned to revising *1984*; by the end of 1948, it was finished, and Orwell was back in a sanatorium following another severe tubercular attack. Secker and Warburg agreed to publish the novel and, like *Animal Farm*, it was chosen as an American Book-of-the-Month Club selection, guaranteeing high sales.

Perhaps Orwell's failing health was taking a toll on his temperament as well. He had always been flexible with his publishers, revising as needed to get his books into print. But with *1984*, perhaps the culmination of his political and literary development, he refused. Book-of-the-Month wanted him to cut two philosophical sections it felt would reduce the book's appeal to an American audience, but Orwell wrote to his agent, "A book is built up as a balanced structure and one cannot simply remove large chunks here and there unless one is ready to recast the whole thing. . . . I really cannot allow my work to be mucked about beyond a certain point." This sentiment reflected not only Orwell's unwillingness to cooperate but the care he took in his writing. The words did not simply roll off his pen, despite what his colleague George Woodcock had observed at *Tribune*. Every word was conceived with care, as was the organizational structure into which he put them. Even in the *Tribune* days, Orwell did significant structural work, through his monologues in the presence of his colleagues.

## MARRIAGE

In the spring of 1949, Sonia Brownell visited Orwell at Cranham, the Gloucestershire sanatorium where he was staying. Just as Orwell was attracted to her youth and vitality, she was attracted to his growing literary reputation. She began visiting him fairly regularly, and he soon proposed. In addition to admiring her, he was confident that her experience in the publishing world would make her an excellent executor of his literary estate. At first Sonia put him off, but by July she had said yes.

Her friend Diana Witherby told biographer Michael Shelden that while Sonia had admired Orwell, she had not loved him. "She could see that she made him happy," Witherby said, "and making him happy made her happy. She liked that, though it was never a case of actually being in love with him."

By September, Orwell's health had so declined as to require hospitalization. He was sent to University College Hospital in London. On October 13, he married Sonia in a bedside hospital ceremony. Orwell wore a red smoking jacket he had sent a friend out to purchase; Sonia and the other few guests went out to celebrate after the ceremony.

Sonia and Orwell planned to go to another sanatorium, this time in Switzerland, in late January 1950. Four days before their scheduled departure date, shortly after midnight on January 21, Orwell died alone in his hospital bed.

## ORWELL'S LEGACY

In 1946, Eric Blair, better known as George Orwell, a man whose powerful writing is still remembered a half century after his death, wrote in his diary:

> There has literally been not one day in which I did not feel that I was idling, that I was behind with the current job, & that my total output was miserably small. Even at the periods when I was working 10 hours a day on a book, or turning out 4 or 5 articles a week, I have never been able to get away from this neurotic feeling.

Always his own harshest critic, Orwell was praised by many. Laurence Brander wrote in his critical biography *George Orwell,*

> Orwell helped to carry on two great traditions in English prose. He was an individualist and he cared for prose style. He did his work at a time when individualism was as unpopular as ever and when more crude writing than ever before was getting into print. . . . Orwell managed [the English language] with great skill. . . . He worked on his prose in the furnace of his intellect until it became a clear reflection of his character and what he had to say.

George Orwell is perhaps best remembered for achieving his goal of "[making] political writing into an art." Few writers have made such an impact on generations of people as Orwell did with his novels *Animal Farm* and *1984.* His portrayal of power misused, working people betrayed, individualism stamped out, and thought manipulated cannot be forgotten. Orwell was, as critic V.S. Pritchett wrote in an obituary, "the wintry conscience of a generation."

# CHAPTER 1

# First Response: The Reviews

READINGS ON ANIMAL FARM

# *Animal Farm* Is a Shallow, Disappointing Novel

Isaac Rosenfeld

When *Animal Farm* was published in the United
States in 1946, it became a runaway best-seller, providing Orwell with the first real financial success he
had achieved as a writer. It became a Book-of-the-
Month Club selection, going out to millions of main-
stream American readers. American critics, too,
mostly praised the book. Isaac Rosenfeld, critic for
the political weekly the *Nation*, was an exception.
While most praised the book either for its quality as
a fable or as a political satire about the Soviet Union,
Rosenfeld said the book doesn't nearly reach its potential: It only skims the surface of what is necessary
to truly compare human behavior to that of animals,
and its theme is likewise too easy and superficial.

Rosenfeld unfavorably compares *Animal Farm* to another powerful political novel of the day, Arthur Koestler's
*Darkness at Noon*. Koestler, a Hungarian-born Zionist, disillusioned Communist, journalist, and novelist, eventually
moved to England, where he continued to write thought-
provoking works until his death in 1983. Like Orwell, he
served in the Spanish Civil War, and in fact, the two men
knew and were influenced by each other. Both were swept
up by the magnificent and romantic idealism of early communism, and both were seriously disillusioned when the
Stalinist purges took place in the 1930s.

*Darkness at Noon* is set in a fictional totalitarian country
and portrays the destruction of a minor official caught in
the web woven by the all-invasive prison state. While there
are definite thematic similarities between *Darkness at Noon*
and *Animal Farm*, the two writers set quite different scopes
for themselves in these novels. Orwell called his "a Fairy

From Isaac Rosenfeld, "Review of *Animal Farm*." Reprinted with permission from the
September 9, 1946, issue of the *Nation* magazine.

Tale," while Koestler's was a full-blown novel. Isaac Rosenfeld felt that *Animal Farm* fails, through its "middle of the way imagination, working with ideas that have only a halfway scope." Such a work, he says, "cannot seriously deal with events [taking place in totalitarian countries and even so-called democratic ones] that are themselves extreme."

George Orwell, to judge by his writing, is a man, not without imagination, who is never swept away by his imagination. His work as a literary critic and analyst of politics and popular culture runs along a well laid out middle course, kept true to it by an even keel; it is always very satisfying, except when he ventures out into certain waters, as in his reflections on art and poetry in his 'Dickens, Dali, and Others,' where a deep keel has the advantage over an even one. Even when he is wrong as he was many times during the war in his political comments and predictions, he is wrong in a sensible way. He stands for a common sense and a reasonableness which are rare today, especially when these virtues are removed from the commonplace, as they are in Orwell's case, though not absolutely.

## A BARNYARD HISTORY

*Animal Farm,* a brief barnyard history of the Russian Revolution from October to just beyond the Stalin-Hitler pact, is the characteristic product of such a mind, both with credit and discredit to its qualities. It puts an imaginative surface on the facts, but does not go far beneath the surface and shows little in excess of the minimum of invention necessary to make the transposition into an animal perspective. The facts are straight, and all the wieldy ones are there; the interpretation, within these limits, is plain and true. The implicit moral attitude toward the real historical events is one of an indignation that goes-without-saying, opposed to the nonsense and chicanery of Party dialectics, and to what has come to be recognized, to a large extent through Orwell's writing, as the well-intentioned, peculiarly liberal act of submission to the tyrant's myth. At least by implication, Orwell again makes clear in this book his allegiance to an older and more honorable liberalism that still holds as its dearest thing the right to liberty of judgment. Nevertheless, this is a disappointing piece of work; its best effort is exerted somewhere on middle ground, between the chuckle-headed monstrosity of orthodox Stalinism and the sated anti-Stalinist intelligence of long standing which already knows all this and a good deal more besides.

In brief, old Major, the pig, shortly before his death, delivers himself of the lessons of his life for the benefit of the animals of Mr Jones's Manor Farm, pointing out to them how they have been exploited by Man (capitalism) and urging the revolutionary establishment of a better society (The Communist Manifesto). The animals drive Mr Jones off the farm and hold it against his attempts to regain possession (Revolution and defeat of the Counter-revolution). Led by two pigs, Napoleon (Stalin), more or less in the background, and Snowball (Trotsky, with a soupçon of Lenin—for simplicity's sake, Vladimir Ilyitch is left out of the picture, entering it only as a *dybbuk* [Yiddish for an evil spirit] who shares with Marx old Major's identity, and with Trotsky, Snowball's) the animals institute a regime free of Man, based on collective ownership, socialized production, equality, etc. The pigs, who are the most intelligent animals, form a bureaucracy which does not at first enjoy many privileges, this development being held over until the factional dispute over the rate of industrialization and the strategy of World Revolution begins, Snowball-Trotsky is exiled, and Napoleon-Stalin comes to power. Then we have, in their animal equivalent, the important episodes of hardship and famine, growth of nationalism, suspension of workers' rights and privileges, frame-ups, Moscow Trials, fake confessions, purges, philosophical revisions—'All animals are equal' becoming, 'All animals are equal, but some animals are more equal than others'—the Stalin-Hitler pact, etc.—all of which is more interesting as an exercise in identification than as a story in its own right.

What I found most troublesome was the question that attended my reading—what is the point of *Animal Farm*? Is it that the pigs, with the most piggish pig supreme, will always disinherit the sheep and the horses? If so, why bother with a debunking fable; why not . . . give assent to the alleged historical necessity? But it is not so. . . . And if we are not to draw the moldy moral of the pig, what then?

## FAILURE OF THE IMAGINATION

Though Orwell, I am sure, would not seriously advance the bad-man theory of history, it appears that he has, nevertheless, drawn on it for the purpose of writing *Animal Farm*. There are only two motives operating in the parable (which is already an oversimplification to the point of falsity, if we take the parable as intended); one of them, a good one, Snowball's, is defeated, and the only other, the bad one, Napoleon's, succeeds, presumably because history belongs to the most unscrupulous. I do not take this to be Orwell's own position, for his work has shown that he knows it to be false and a waste of time in historical analysis; it is, however, the position of his imagination, as divorced from what he knows—a convenient ground, itself a fable, to set his fable on. (If Marxism has really failed, the most ironic thing about its failure is that it should be attributed to the piggishness of human nature.) It is at this point that a failure of imagination—failure to expand the parable, to incorporate into it something of the complexity of the real event—becomes identical with a failure in politics. The story, which is inadequate as a way into the reality, also falls short as a way out; and while no one has a right to demand of *Animal Farm* that it provide a solution to the Russian problem—something it never set out to do—it is nevertheless true that its political relevance is more apparent than real. It will offer a kind of enlightenment to those who still need it, say, the members of the Book of the Month Club, but beyond this it has no politics at all.

## A BACKWARD WORK

Another way of making this point is to compare *Animal Farm* with [Arthur] Koestler's *Darkness at Noon*. Rubashov, also faced with the triumph of the pig, at least asks *why* the pig is so attractive, *why* he wins out over the good. This is a question that can no longer be answered by stating *that* the pig wins out. It is a more sophisticated question, for it realizes that the fact of the triumph is already known, and a more important one, for it leads to an examination of the pig's supremacy along two divergent lines, by way of a specific Marxist analysis of history, or a criticism of Marxism in general, both engaging the imagination at a crucial point. But Orwell's method, of taking a well worn fact that we know and converting it, for lack of better inspiration, into an imaginative symbol, actually falsifies the fact; thus over-extended, the fact of Stalinist 'human nature,' the power-drive of the bureaucracy, ceases to explain anything, and even makes one forget what it is to which it does apply. An indication that a middle of the way imagination, working with ideas that have only a half-way scope, cannot seriously deal with events that are themselves extreme. There is, however, some value in the method of *Animal Farm,* provided it is timely, in the sense, not of newspapers, but of history, in advance of the news. But this is to say that *Animal Farm* should have been written years ago; coming as it does, in the wake of the event, it can only be called a backward work.

# *Animal Farm* Is a Powerful and Sad Fable

Graham Greene

George Orwell received several rejections, even from publishers he had successfully worked with in the past, before he finally found a publisher for *Animal Farm*. The franker publishers told him that the novel was not right for the times, that it treated too sensitive a topic in too bold a manner; it did, after all, openly criticize the Soviet Union, one of the Allies during World War II. Once published, however, the book received many positive reviews, including one by Graham Greene.

Greene, himself a noted novelist, essayist, and playwright, frequently wrote about the human inability to overcome evil, whether it was within an individual or a government. Several of Greene's many admired novels (among them *The Third Man*, 1950; *A Burnt-Out Case*, 1961; and *The Honorary Consul*, 1973) were set in the midst of governmental intrigue. Greene was also a strong moralist. These traits made him uniquely qualified to comment on George Orwell's moralistic political satire *Animal Farm*. In his review, Greene focuses on the integrity of the novelist, who, he says, paints a true picture of a sad and dangerous situation that politicians hypocritically gloss over in order to be "diplomatic" with a past and perhaps future ally.

Whatever you may say about writers—their private lives, their feeding habits or their taste in shirts—you have to admit, I think, that there has never been such a thing as a literature of appeasement.

Writers may pass, like everyone else, through the opium dream of Munich and Yalta, but no literature comes out of

From Graham Greene, "*Animal Farm*," Review, Evening Standard (London), August 10, 1945. Reprinted courtesy of International Creative Management, New York, and David Higham Associates, London, as agents for the author's estate.

that dream.

For literature is concerned above everything else with the accurate expression of a personal vision, while appeasement is a matter of compromise.

Nevertheless, in wartime there has to be a measure of appeasement, and it is as well for the writer to keep quiet. He must not give way to despondency or dismay, he must not offend a valuable ally, he must not even make fun. . . .

It is a welcome sign of peace that Mr George Orwell is able to publish his 'fairy story' *Animal Farm,* a satire upon the totalitarian state and one state in particular. I have heard a rumour that the manuscript was at one time submitted to the Ministry of Information, that huge cenotaph of appeasement, and an official there took a poor view of it. 'Couldn't you make them some other animal,' he is reported as saying in reference to the dictator and his colleagues, 'and not pigs?'

For this is the story of a political experiment on a farm where the animals, under the advice of a patriarchal porker, get organised and eventually drive out Mr Jones, the human owner.

The porker does not live to see the success of his revolution, but two other pigs, Snowball and Napoleon, soon impose their leadership on the farm animals. Never had the farm animals worked with such elan for Mr Jones as they now work, so they believe, for themselves. They have a song, 'Beasts of England'; they have the inspiring seven commandments of Animalism, taught them by the old porker, painted on the barn for all to see.

1. Whoever goes upon two legs is an enemy.
2. Whatever goes upon four legs, or has wings, is a friend.
3. No animal shall wear clothes.
4. No animal shall sleep in a bed.
5. No animal shall drink alcohol.
6. No animal shall kill any other animal.
7. All animals are equal.

They have a banner which blows over the farmhouse garden, a hoof and horn in white painted on an old green tablecloth.

## A SAD FABLE

It is a sad fable, and it is an indication of Mr Orwell's fine talent that it is really sad—not a mere echo of human failings at one remove. We do become involved in the fate of Molly the Cow, old Benjamin the Donkey, and Boxer the poor devil of a hard-working, easily deceived Horse. Snowball is driven out by Napoleon, who imposes his solitary leadership with the help of a gang of savage dogs, and slowly the Seven Commandments become altered or erased, until at last on the barn door appears only one sentence. 'All animals are equal, but some animals are more equal than others.'

If Mr Walt Disney is looking for a real subject, here it is: it has all the necessary humour, and it has, too, the subdued lyrical quality he can sometimes express so well. But is it perhaps a little too real for him? There is no appeasement here.

> As for the others, their life, so far as they knew, was as it had always been. They were generally hungry, they slept on straw, they drank from the pool, they laboured in the fields; in winter they were troubled by the cold, and in summer by the flies. Sometimes the older ones among them racked their dim memories and tried to determine whether in the early days of the Rebellion, when Jones's expulsion was still recent, things had been better or worse than now. They could not remember. . . . Only old Benjamin professed to remember every detail of his long life and to know that things never had been, nor ever could be much better or much worse—hunger, hardship, and disappointment being, so he said, the unalterable law of life.

# *Animal Farm* Is an Amusing and Alarming Novel

Louis M. Ridenour

*Animal Farm* was well received in America, where it was published in 1946. Had the book been published two years earlier, when the United States was strongly allied with the Soviet Union in the effort to stop Hitler, reception might not have been so friendly. By 1946, however, the war was over, American soldiers were home, and Americans were feeling more carefree; at the same time they were waking up to newly perceived dangers emanating from the USSR.

*Saturday Review,* one of the country's most popular literary weeklies, was among those that enthusiastically praised *Animal Farm.* Critic Louis M. Ridenour stated in the *Review* that the book was both amusing and alarming. Ridenour, like many other readers, was captivated by the novel's fairy-tale form, even as he perceived a deeper, darker message.

George Orwell's "Animal Farm" is intrinsically a very amusing book. It deals only incidentally with animals and farms; it is an extended allegory dealing with the history of the Soviet Union. Even a reader as ignorant of the detailed history of Russia as I am can spot the Bolshevik revolution, the early successes of the Red Army, the excommunication of Trotsky (who seems to be a pig named Snowball), the growth of the internal Terror, the various industrial Five-Year Plans, the Russo-German pact and its breakdown, and similar prominent landmarks. No doubt there are a great many minor parallels which will not be lost on a reader who is well informed in terms of Soviet history.

The book is a splendid technical job, whose easy and di-

From Louis M. Ridenour, "Allegory with Goose Pimples," Review, *Saturday Review,* August 24, 1946.

verting style never once lags from beginning to end. It is no simple matter to sustain a fable like this one for more than a hundred pages, and Mr. Orwell does it admirably. He does it, apparently, with two main purposes in view. The first is to amuse; the transposition of human actions and attitudes into the antics of non-human animals has been a good dodge since Aesop. On the other hand, the author satirizes the communist state. Much of his attention is devoted to showing how the grand promises of the early days have been compromised by expediency and dissipated by the growth of personal ambition and love of power among the pigs who lead Mr. Orwell's miniature communist state.

The writing of "Animal Farm" was finished in February, 1944. I dare say that if I had read it then, or within eighteen months of that time, I should have thought it extremely funny, and I should have been greatly impressed by the way in which the book points up the major current weakness of the Soviet Union—that it is a tyranny of the blackest sort. I should have generated a complacency concerning our own form of government by considering the drawbacks of a different rule which pretends to be devoted even more thoroughly to the rights of the common man. In the context of today, "Animal Farm," although still intrinsically amusing, carries a most alarming reminder.

## Modern History Flattens Humor

Like a number of old ideas, several naval vessels, and more than a hundred thousand people, my ability to derive unconcerned amusement from "Animal Farm" is a casualty of the atomic bomb: The increasingly tyrannous doings of the pigs who run the farm seem far more ominous than funny at a time when we must deal with the pigs in an atmosphere of flawless reciprocal trust or all perish together.

Nothing but the lust of men for power over other men, and the xenophobia generated by that lust, seems today to stand in the way of the creation of firm and workable arrangements for the worldwide control of atomic energy. The price of failure is clear; yet the efforts for world organization and peace may fail.

On Memorial Drive in Cambridge, a few nights ago, my daughter, who is not quite six, noticed the monument which marks the landing of the Norsemen on this continent a thousand years ago. I told her what it was for. She said, "If there

## You Can't Categorize Orwell

*The following comment comes from an essay Jonah Raskin, a California professor, wrote for* Monthly Review, *an American Socialist journal. Raskin points out that George Orwell was not easy to pigeonhole.*

Taken as a whole, Orwell's legacy is profoundly contradictory. Unpredictable and iconoclastic, he was a maverick to his dying day.

Orwell took sides and changed sides dramatically. He joined the Imperial Police in Burma and resigned from the Imperial Police, disgusted with the white man's job in the East. He went to Spain to fight against fascism, was wounded by a fascist sniper, but fled from Spain dedicated to fighting against communism. Strongly opinionated, Orwell reserved the right to change his opinions whenever he saw fit. ("Fascism and bourgeois 'democracy' are Tweedledum and Tweedledee," he wrote in 1937. And shortly thereafter he complained, "You can only pretend that Nazism and capitalist democracy are Tweedledum and Tweedledee.")

Orwell insisted on the necessity of taking sides, but at the same time he believed that it was futile to take sides. "By fighting against the bourgeoisie," he wrote in 1936, "a working man . . . becomes bourgeois." Moreover, Orwell had a perverse habit of admiring the side he opposed and detesting the side he supported. An anti-fascist, he had a fascist streak in him. In a 1940 review of *Mein Kampf,* he wrote, "I have never been able to dislike Hitler. Ever since he came to power . . . I have reflected that I would certainly kill him if I could get within reach of him, but that I feel no personal animosity. The fact is that there is something deeply appealing about him.". . .

In many ways the labels "reactionary" and "progressive" don't fit Orwell. He defined himself as a "Tory anarchist," a contradiction in terms, but still it is a useful handle. The anarchist Orwell hated authorities and orthodoxies, and celebrated the autonomous individual. The Tory Orwell respected tradition, continuity, community. He loved the earth, its peoples and cultures, from Burma to Morocco, Catalonia to London. Orwell hated modern society with its television, glib magazines, Hollywood movies, chain bookstores, and piped-in music. He identified with the "down and out" and hungered for old-fashioned, remote, uncommercial cultures. In that sense he was a "reactionary," but a "reactionary" who wanted to protect the world that the neoconservatives would annex, pillage, plunder, destroy.

had been some Americans here then, they would have fought them off."

When a child picks up this sort of reasoning—God knows how, I suppose by osmosis—before she can read and write, and when it is clear that such an approach to world problems will mean the destruction of us all, it is difficult to be amused by the moral decline of some pigs debauched by power over their barnyard fellows. No doubt I have got atoms before my eyes, and ought to be able to dissociate world problems from a simple rural allegory, but I can't. In the last war I saw fairly extensively what chemical explosives can do, and as a scientist I have had some training in appreciating the significance of the factor of a million which separates these chemical explosives from the new explosives we now know how to make. When pigs act like people, or people act like pigs (depending on how you look at it), I am disturbed, for I know what is at stake.

If the carefree humor of "Animal Farm" is gone, then, the biting satire remains. My own pleasure in this satire is greatly reduced by my realization that its object is, as usual, far less the communist system than the nature of man himself as this nature has been revealed in the latter-day development of the communist system. It is easy to admire the superb craftsmanship with which the attack is carried out, but it is not comfortable to contemplate the probable results, in terms of future history, of the traits of human character elaborated in the satire.

The message of "Animal Farm" seems to be, not that Russia's leaders have enslaved and exploited their people, though perhaps they have, but that people are no damn good.

# CHAPTER 2

# *Animal Farm* as Literature

# *Animal Farm* Is a Successful Animal Fable

Christopher Hollis

"The world is full of animal fables in which this or that country is symbolized by this or that animal, and very tedious affairs the greater number of them are," writes politician, author, and Catholic intellectual Christopher Hollis. In contrast to these, *Animal Farm* is a masterpiece, he asserts. Orwell's old Eton schoolmate, who more frequently criticized Orwell than praised him, favorably compares this short novel to the 2,500-year-old animal fables of the Greek slave Aesop, the Frenchman La Fontaine's seventeenth-century fables, and even the animal tales of the fourteenth-century English storyteller Geoffrey Chaucer. All of these men's moralistic tales could be said to be timeless—we are still reading, retelling, and taking lessons from them centuries after their creators' demises. Hollis seems to think the same fate may await *Animal Farm*.

He suggests that Orwell had a dark message for the twentieth century that would not have been accepted had he simply preached it. By couching it in terms of a simple, lighthearted "fairy tale," he could pass his message on without alienating his readers, readers who were weary of the darkness of World War II and ready to move into a newer, happier, more optimistic age, but readers who, Orwell believed, needed to be warned to be vigilant against a future controlled by power-hungry rulers.

Whatever the advantages or disadvantages of the German invasion of Russia, at least it saved Britain from the risk of immediate invasion and defeat, and thus such a man as Orwell, who was alarmed at the ultimate consequences of the

Excerpted from Christopher Hollis, *A Study of George Orwell: The Man and His Works* (London: Hollis & Carter, 1956).

Russian alliance, was able to live his life under a lesser strain in the last years of the war than in the first. He was able to give his mind once more to creative writing. Yet the problem what to write was not simple. The crying need to his mind was to arouse public opinion to the dangers of the Russian alliance. Yet the mood of the country at the time when Stalingrad was being defended was not such that it would tolerate a straightforward and bitter attack on Russia—the kind of attack which he had already launched in his essay in the composite volume, the *Betrayal of the Left*, which he had published in 1941, when of course public opinion in Britain was willing to tolerate it because Russia was still bound in hostility to us by the Nazi-Soviet Pact. Now direction could only be found out by indirection. The consequence, immediately and apparently inconvenient to Orwell as a writer, turned out in the event to be brilliantly fortunate. For it caused Orwell to make his point by the indirect, roundabout, whimsical road of an animal fairy-story and thus led him to experiment with a new form of writing of which he proved himself magnificently the master. Whereas his previous books had never had more than small and struggling sales, *Animal Farm* at once caught the public fancy in almost every country of the world—particularly in the United States—was translated into every one of the leading languages, established him as one of the best-selling authors of the day and incidentally gave him for the first time in life a tolerable income. . . .

## THE FABLE'S MEANING

The interpretation of the fable is plain enough. Major, Napoleon, Snowball—Lenin, Stalin and Trotzky—Pilkington and Frederick, the two groups of non-Communist powers— the Marxian thesis, as expounded by Major, that society is divided into exploiters and exploited and that all the exploited need to do is to rise up, to expel the exploiters and seize the 'surplus value' which the exploiters have previously annexed to themselves—the Actonian thesis that power corrupts and the Burnhamian thesis that the leaders of the exploited, having used the rhetoric of equality to get rid of the old exploiters, establish in their place not a classless society but themselves as a new governing class—the greed and unprincipled opportunism of the non-Communist states, which are ready enough to overthrow the Communists by force so long as they imagine that their overthrow will be easy but begin to talk of peace when they find the task difficult and when they think that they can use the Communists to satisfy their greed—the dishonour among total thugs, as a result of which, though greed may make original ideology irrelevant, turning pigs into men and men into pigs, the thugs fall out among themselves, as the Nazis and the Communists fell out, not through difference of ideology but because in a society of utter baseness and insincerity there is no motive of confidence. The interpretation is so plain that no serious critic can dispute it. Those Russian critics who have professed to see in it merely a general satire on bureaucracy without any special reference to any particular country can hardly be taken seriously.

Yet even a total acceptance of Orwell's political opinions would not in itself make *Animal Farm* a great work of art. The world is full of animal fables in which this or that country is symbolized by this or that animal, and very tedious affairs the greater number of them are—and that, irrespective of whether we agree or disagree with their opinions. To be a great book, a book of animal fables requires literary greatness as well as a good cause. Such greatness *Animal Farm* surely possesses. As Orwell fairly claimed, *Animal Farm* 'was the first book in which I tried, with full consciousness of what I was doing, to fuse political purpose and artistic purpose into one whole'—and he succeeded.

The problems that are set by this peculiar form of art, which makes animals behave like human beings, are clear. The writer must throughout be successful in preserving a delicate and whimsical balance. As Johnson truly says in his criticism of Dryden's *Hind and the Panther*, there is an initial absurdity in making animals discuss complicated intellectual problems—the nature of the Church's authority in Dryden's case, the communist ideology in Orwell's. The absurdity can only be saved from ridicule if the author is able to couch his argument in very simple terms and to draw his illustrations from the facts of animal life. In this Orwell is as successful as he could be—a great deal more successful incidentally than Dryden, who in the excitement of the argument often forgets that it is animals who are supposed to be putting it forward. The practical difficulties of the conceit must either be ignored or apparently solved in some simple and striking—if possible, amusing—fashion. Since obviously they could not in reality be solved at all, the author merely makes himself ridiculous if he allows himself to get bogged down in tedious and detailed explanations which at the end of all cannot in the nature of things explain anything. Thus Orwell is quite right merely to ignore the difficulties of language, to assume that the animals can communicate with one another by speech—or to assume that the new ordinance which forbids any animal to take another animal's life could

### A Simple, Relentless Allegory

*Jenni Calder, the author of many literary studies, discusses what makes* Animal Farm *a successful allegory.*

The allegory is very precise in its use of the major figures and incidents of the Russian Revolution. It expresses quite nakedly and with a complete lack of intellectual argument those aspects of Stalinism that most disturbed Orwell. At the same time the humbleness and warmth of the narrative give an attractive obliqueness without turning the direction of the satire. We can feel compassion for Orwell's creatures in a way that we cannot for Winston Smith, for the stark narrative of *Nineteen Eighty-Four* stuns our capacity for reaction. But *Animal Farm* is equally relentless in its message. The relentless quality is partly contained in the even tone of the language. In the midst of describing hardship and disaster it does not vary—it matches the pathetic doggedness of the animals themselves. In no other work does Orwell so successfully resist the temptation to launch into barely relevant side issues. The measured amalgam of straightforward vocabulary and colloquial phrase has a strange power, perhaps because Orwell writes with a complete lack of self-consciousness, as if he were describing recognised facts, and without the pretense of inserting himself into the animals' minds.

Orwell identifies himself with the animals while maintaining his distance, in the same way as he identified himself with tramps or the unemployed. His sympathetic detachment reinforces the plain strength of the prose. The words are simple, the sentences short, many with only a single clause. The simplicity gives an authentic quality to the writing. As in so much of Orwell's writing he does not erect clusters of words and phrases which come between him and his reader and disguise meaning rather than illuminate it. Adjectives like "harsh and bare," "cold," "hungry" do all the work that is needed without embroidery, although they are the kind of adjectives that often become removed from their plain meanings.

be applied with only the comparatively mild consequence of gradual increase in animal population. He is justified in telling us the stories of the two attacks by men for the recapture of the Farm but in refusing to spoil his story by allowing the men to take the full measures which obviously men would take if they found themselves in such an impossible situation. The means by which the animals rout the men are inevitably signally unconvincing if we are to consider them seriously at all. It would as obviously be ridiculous to delay for pages to describe how animals build windmills or how they write up commandments on a wall. It heightens the comedy to give a passing sentence of description to their hauling the stone up a hill so that it may be broken into manageable fractions when it falls over the precipice, or to Squealer, climbing a ladder to paint up his message.

## THE ANIMAL FABLE MUST BE LIGHT-HEARTED

The animal fable, if it is to succeed at all, ought clearly to carry with it a gay and light-hearted message. It must be full of comedy and laughter. The form is too far removed from reality to tolerate sustained bitterness. Both Chaucer and La Fontaine discovered this in their times, and the trouble with Orwell was that the lesson which he wished to teach was not ultimately a gay lesson. It was not the lesson that mankind had its foibles and its follies but that all would be well in the end. It was more nearly a lesson of despair—the lesson that anarchy was intolerable, that mankind could not be ruled without entrusting power somewhere or other and, to whomsoever power was entrusted, it was almost certain to be abused. For power was itself corrupting. But it was Orwell's twisted triumph that in the relief of the months immediately after the war mankind was probably not prepared to take such dark medicine if it had been offered to it undiluted. It accepted it because it came in this gay and coloured and fanciful form.

The film version gives to *Animal Farm* a happy ending. The animals all the world over, hearing how Napoleon has betrayed the animal cause, rise up against him at the end and in a second revolution expel him. After this second revolution, we are left to believe, a rule of freedom and equality is established and survives. But of course this ending makes nonsense of the whole thesis. It was the Orwellian thesis, right or wrong, that power inevitably corrupts and that revolutions therefore inevitably fail of their purpose. The new masters are necessarily corrupted by their new power. The second revolution would necessarily have failed of its purpose just as the first had failed. It would merely have set up a second vicious circle.

*Animal Farm* possesses two essential qualities of a successful animal fable. On the one hand the author of such a fable must have the Swift-like capacity of ascribing with solemn face to the animals idiotic but easily recognized human qualities, decking them out in aptly changed phraseology to suit the animal life—ascribe the quality and then pass quickly on before the reader has begun to find the point overlaboured. This Orwell has to perfection. Thus:

> Snowball also busied himself with organizing the other animals into what he called Animal Committees. He was indefatigable at this. He formed the Egg Production Committee for the hens, the Clean Tails League for the cows, the Wild Comrades' Re-education Committee (the object of which was to tame the cats and rabbits), the Whiter Wool Movement for the sheep, and various others, besides instituting classes in reading and writing. On the whole these projects were a failure. The attempt to tame the wild creatures, for instance, broke down almost immediately. They continued to behave very much as before and, when treated with generosity, simply took advantage of it. The cat joined the Re-education Committee and was very active in it for some days. She was seen one day sitting on a roof talking to some sparrows who were just out of reach. She was telling them that all animals were now comrades and that any sparrow who chose could come and perch on her paw; but the sparrows kept their distance.

Or:

> When the laws of Animal Farm were first formulated, the retiring age had been fixed for horses and pigs at twelve, for cows at fourteen, for dogs at nine, for sheep at seven and for hens and geese at five. Liberal old-age pensions had been agreed upon. As yet no animal had actually retired on a pension, but of late the subject had been discussed more and more. Now that the small field beyond the orchard had been set aside for barley, it was rumoured that a corner of the large pasture was to be fenced off and turned into a grazing-ground for superannuated animals. For a horse, it was said, the pension would be five pounds of corn a day and, in winter, fifteen pounds of hay, with a carrot or possibly an apple on public holidays.

## LOVE OF ANIMALS

But what is also essential—and this is often overlooked—is that the writer should have himself a genuine love of animals—should be able to create here and there, in the midst of all his absurdity, scenes of animal life, in themselves re- alistic and lovable. In that Chaucer, the first and greatest of Orwell's masters in this form of art, pre-eminently excelled. It was in that that Orwell himself excelled. He had always been himself a lover of animals, intimate with their ways. 'Most of the good memories of my childhood, and up to the age of about twenty,' he wrote in *Such, Such were the Joys*, 'are in some way connected with animals', and it was the work with animals which attracted him in maturer years to agricultural life. There is a real poetic quality, mixed whim- sically in with absurdity, in his picture of the first meeting of the animals in the barn with which the book opens.

# *Animal Farm* Is Trivial

Keith Alldritt

Most readers agree that *Animal Farm* is an easy
book to read and understand. But is this ease a
virtue or a fault? Keith Alldritt, professor of English
at the University of Vancouver, asserts that it is the
latter. He suggests that the simplicity of the book by-
passes the serious impact and emotions that the subject matter is worthy of. It is a "turning away from
the disturbing complexities of the experience rather
than . . . confronting them." Where some see a clever
and effective way of warning readers about the dangers of totalitarianism, Alldritt sees facile shallowness. Alldritt has written several books on history
and literature.

Orwell became famous with the publication of *Animal Farm*
in 1945. Upon this book, together with *Nineteen Eighty-Four*
and the essays, his reputation continues chiefly to rest.
Today it is very difficult to share the admiration with which
*Animal Farm* was received when it first appeared. All the
comparisons with *Gulliver's Travels* and *Candide* that are to
be found in the contemporary reviews must now seem,
twenty years on, extremely damaging to Orwell's book. And
only when we recall that its publication coincided with the
beginning of the Cold War does its instant success become
understandable. Certainly as a mocking allegory of the first
thirty years or so of the Russian revolution it is a work of
considerable poise, a poise that derives from Orwell's long
nurtured cynicism about communism, which had resisted
the indulgent attitude to Russia born of the war-time alliance
as much as it had resisted the fashionable communism of literary and intellectual circles during the thirties. But for the
reader of today it is this very poise which makes the book
trivial. The allegory is too pat, the confidence of the narrator
(the confidence of one telling a nursery tale) too secure. Or-

Excerpted from Keith Alldritt, *The Making of George Orwell: An Essay in Literary History* (London: Edward Arnold, 1969). Copyright ©1969 by Keith Alldritt. Reprinted by permission of Edward Arnold Ltd.

well's "fairy story" is only a clever form for expressing a set of opinions that have been held so long that they no longer admit the complexity of the experience they claim to explain.

## ANIMAL FARM AND THE SPANISH WAR

The story of the humanised beasts of *Animal Farm* treats of events that are in many ways similar to those in which Orwell himself had participated in Spain. As in *Homage to Catalonia,* we have an account of a revolution created by a community undergoing persecution and deprivation. But idealism and communal energy and purpose do not long endure, we are told again, and the selfish and the unscrupulous take over the revolution and recreate the same sort of class system and exploitation which the revolution had overthrown. It is a measure of the poverty of *Animal Farm* that it does little more than rehearse these "points." In *Homage to Catalonia* such conclusions were merely one part of an intense and movingly evoked experience. But in *Animal Farm* they form the totality of what the book has to offer us. We may perhaps derive some pleasure from elucidating the allegory. We may identify old Major, the aged porker who has the dream and who provides the ideological impulse to the revolution, as Karl Marx, and we may recognise the quarrel between Napoleon and Snowball as representing the rift between Stalin and Trotsky. And we may like to find the allegorical counterparts of the treason trials, the emergence of the Soviet secret police, the drive for technological achievement, the perversion of the ideals of the revolution and the misuse of propaganda. Nevertheless, if there is any pleasure in making such discoveries, it is hardly a literary pleasure. Indeed, in specifically literary terms, there is only one aspect of the book that continues to interest us and that is its form, and the particular tone of voice which this form enjoins upon the author. And the form is noteworthy not because of any particular distinction which it involves for the book, but rather because it is Orwell's first renewed effort to solve the problem of form in prose fiction which had been abandoned since the writing of *Coming Up For Air.*

*Animal Farm* is subtitled "A Fairy Story." Since the book does not tell of fairies, nor yet of the magical, this description seems hardly appropriate. Still it does suggest one intention of the book, which is to tell a story directly and simply. In this respect Orwell's purpose is a characteristic one, namely the vigorous sweeping aside of jargon, cant and hypocrisy and the presenting of issues clearly and intelligibly. But this sort of intention always has its attendant dangers and in the telling of his fairy story Orwell has succumbed to them. His account of revolution is greatly oversimplified; it is too obvious, too facile, too easy. For whatever we may think of the Russian revolution or, for that matter of any revolution, we cannot but be aware that the crises of a society are much more complex than Orwell is here able to suggest. And the feelings about revolution which the book elicits are as unsophisticated as the narrative itself. Take, for instance, the emotional climax of the book which comes when Boxer, the loyal and hard-working but unintelligent work horse, emblematic of "the common people," is sold to the knackers by the pig-commissars when he becomes too ill to work any more. The feelings of simple compassion and absolutely righteous indignation which this incident is calculated to evoke may be tolerable in a nursery tale that has no pretensions to being anything other than a nursery tale. But in one which lays claim to offer the adult intelligence some feeling for the realities of modern social and political life, they cannot, because of their crudity and sentimentality, merit serious attention. At the cost of this sort of oversimplification the sustained poise of the narrative is purchased. Clearly Orwell enjoys the easy confidence to which the position of a teller of nursery tales entitles him. The avuncular security and the poker-faced humour bestowed by the conventions of the form solve completely the difficult problem of the author-reader relationship which in the past had proved so troublesome. But in order to enjoy writing in this way, Orwell has made himself oblivious of the complexity of the experience with which his story purports to deal. He has here found a form which is easy and pleasing to him, but which is a means for turning away from the disturbing complexities of experience rather than for confronting them. It allows only of simple ideas, easy responses and obvious conclusions.

## Too Cozy

This particular form of the nursery story has been borrowed from that cosy world prior to the first World War upon which, as we have seen, Orwell was so ready to dwell. *Animal Farm* especially reminds us of Kipling's stories for children. The laws of the revolution that are painted on the wall of the cowshed and chanted by the animals clearly owe something to "The Law of the Jungle" in Kipling's *Second Jungle Book*. Indeed the central device of *Animal Farm*, the convention of humanised animals, may also derive most immediately from Kipling's *Jungle Book*. And Orwell's narrative tone is obviously modelled on that of the *Just So Stories*. And of course there is the Dickensian element, that traditional element which endures beneath the experimentalism in every one of Orwell's novels and shows the strength of the premodern and the unmodern in his literary sensibility. The humour of the book, when it is not "just so" humour, is Dickensian, achieved by the use of "the unnecessary detail" which Orwell in his critical essay had identified and given examples of and relished as "the unmistakable mark of Dickens's writing." For instance, an important stage in Comrade Napoleon's gradual abandonment of the principles of animalism occurs when he sits down at table to eat. But in relating this, Orwell tells just a little bit more; he "always ate," he tells us, "from the crown Derby dinner service which had been in the glass cupboard in the drawing room." This comic surface of the prose is the major effect of *Animal Farm*. The book is, in fact, a piece of literary self-indulgence. As a writer Orwell has here taken refuge in a simple, comfortable Edwardian form which allows him a perspective upon the modern world and a relationship with his reader which, however relaxed they may be, are neither engaging nor illuminating.

# Politics, Not Literary Quality, Has Made *Animal Farm* a Lasting Novel

Stephen Sedley

Stephen Sedley is a British attorney (queen's counsel), poet, translator, and critic. In the following article, he comments on the long tradition of teaching *Animal Farm* in literature classes. Upon reflection, he finds it rather strange, for, he says, there are far better examples of literature using a human-animal analogy as their basis. The stories written by Beatrix Potter, author of the charming tales of Peter Rabbit and his friends, and Kenneth Grahame, author of the classic story *The Wind in the Willows*, were far more successful in attributing human characteristics to animals, and they were more entertaining as well. These stories also manage to say something about the state of society. *Animal Farm*, in contrast, he says, is shallow and simplistic.

Imaginative literature does not have to justify itself politically. On the contrary, part of its value may be to enhance or modify its readers' political comprehension. Marx's well-known preference for Balzac, a royalist, over Zola, a socialist, makes the point well enough, but it is or ought to be the experience of every socialist that it is not shared assumptions but shared experience that makes good literature a humanising and encouraging force.

Re-reading *Animal Farm* a generation after I first encountered it—as you my reader probably did—on the school curriculum, I am struck by its distance from any of these considerations. It lacks, deliberately, any effort to draw the reader into a convincing fiction, to invite a willing suspen-

From Stephen Sedley, "An Immodest Proposal: Animal Farm," in *Inside the Myth: Orwell: Views from the Left*, edited by Christopher Norris (London: Lawrence & Wishart, 1984). Copyright © Stephen Sedley. Reprinted by permission of the publisher.

sion of disbelief. Instead it demands assent to its major premise that people in their political lives can be equated with domesticated animals, and to its minor premise that civil society, like a farm, will be run for better or for worse by those who by birth or force inherit power. From these premises the story and its moral follow; without them there is neither story nor moral.

The book is still required reading in most schools . . . but I was interested that my eldest child, a good reader who was given it at the age of thirteen, was bored stiff by it. The reason, it turned out, was that she was too new to political ideas to have any frame of reference for the story: she literally couldn't see what it was about. There was no invitation to enter into the fiction, no common point of departure for reader and writer.

This is certainly not a necessary condition of political allegory or satire: one has to go no farther than Orwell's next major work, *Nineteen Eighty-Four*, to see that. Nor is it a necessary condition of animal fables: our literature is rich in examples. It is an abdication of imaginative art, and one which makes the critical and pedagogic success of *Animal Farm* a sobering example of the substitution of political endorsement for critical appraisal (a vice of which the political right does not have a monopoly).

Orwell's lineage from Swift is frequently spoken of. In background and personality there are similarities, and in some of their writings too, but not in *Animal Farm*. It is not only that Swift has humour as well as passion, which Orwell does not. Swift's satirical method is practically the reverse of Orwell's. Through the picaresque fantasy of *Gulliver's Travels* or the solemn reasoning of *A Modest Proposal* Swift draws the reader down a convincing false trail. The fiction stands, as his contemporaries would have said, on its own bottom. It is only when his readers have passed the point of no return that they realise that they are reading about themselves. But you cannot get into the fiction of *Animal Farm* at all without accepting as your starting point the very thing that Orwell has to prove—that in politics people are no better than animals: their traditional rulers may be feckless but ungovern them and a new tyranny will fill the place of the old. Naturally if you are prepared to accept that conclusion as your premise, the story follows. You can demonstrate that the earth is flat by a similar process.

The use of animals to make a point about people is as old as art itself. Folk literatures abound in animals which are not only human but superhuman. Through them the human endeavour to understand and control the natural and social environments is expressed and developed. You find it in English folk tradition in the ballad of the *Cutty Wren,* the hedge-king; in Irish tradition in *Reynardine,* the man-fox; in Scots tradition in the *Grey Selchie,* the man-seal. In modern English literature we have at least two exponents who show up the poverty of Orwell's creativity, Beatrix Potter and Kenneth Grahame. The best of Beatrix Potter's stories are so well made that it is easy to lose critical perspective in evaluating them. It is enough perhaps to observe how meticulously she invests her animals with sufficient human qualities to enable them to be real characters without ceasing to be animals. Mr. Jackson is a revolting old toad with a toad's predilections in food, but he mimics human character in ways which wryly enlarge your appreciation of human character. The quiet analogy between the amphibious and the human Mr. Jackson neither demands assent to the proposition that there is not much to choose between people and toads nor invites that conclusion. In its small way it is a piece of humane imaginative literature, drawing on the links between human and animal life without straining them.

Perhaps the most indicative contrast is between Potter's and Orwell's versions of the scatter-brained and least rational members of their animal societies—in Potter's books the ducks and rabbits, in Orwell's the sheep. The puddleducks, especially Jemima Puddleduck who nearly gets eaten by the fox in her desire to establish her independence (an interesting parallel with the *Animal Farm* story), are again small mirrors of humanity, pompous and opinionated in proportion to their foolishness. The extended rabbit family is what Beatrix Potter's successors would have regarded as a problem family, delinquents and all, held together by a long-suffering mother. The human presence, Mr. McGregor the grumpy old market gardener, is simply another element of risk in their world: they eat his lettuces and, when he can, he eats them.

In Orwell the silliest of the animals are the sheep. They are the essential and unwitting allies of the tyrant pigs, endlessly bleating the slogan 'Four legs good, two legs bad' in any controversy and drowning all serious discussion. They have no reality as characters, but they do represent the British upper class's opinion of the working class: mindless creatures who do what others direct and bleat what others devise. The remaining farm animals, apart from the pigs, are more or less stupid and more or less good natured. The pigs are cunning and evil.

## POLITICAL ALLEGORY OF THE PIGS

It is in the pigs that the political allegory takes its most precise form. The dream of revolution is dreamt by the old pig Major, who dies before it happens. His manifesto speech to the animals is couched in terms of self-evident absurdity:

> Man is the only real enemy we have. Remove Man from the scene, and the root cause of hunger and overwork is abolished for ever.... No argument must lead you astray. Never listen when they tell you that Man and the animals have a common interest, and that the prosperity of the one is the prosperity of the others. It is all lies.

So it is, we are to understand, with civil society: only a fool could talk like this. (The sidelight this passage throws on Orwell's brand of socialism is interesting.)

To Major's Marx, Napoleon plays Stalin and Snowball Trotsky: the allegory becomes a simple set of personal disguises. The brightest of the other animals, the dogs, are finally bribed and bred into a private army at the pigs' service. The rest, from the willing cart-horses to the fecund hens, are put upon endlessly to keep the pigs in idle comfort.

No honest socialist or communist ignores or underrates the structural and political problems and distortions which have characterised the Soviet Union and other states that have taken a similar path. 'More equal than others' is a barb which has stuck painfully in the consciousness of the left, for the existence of a privileged élite in any socialist state is a fundamental contradiction in political terms. For some on the left it argues that Marxism is not the way to socialism; for some, that Marxism has been betrayed; for some, that Marxism has been vindicated by the state's survival. Not one of these viewpoints, nor any variant of them, is explored or enriched by *Animal Farm*. Orwell's argument is pitched at a different level: it is that socialism in whatever form offers the common people no more hope than capitalism; that it will be first betrayed and then held to ransom by those forces which human beings have in common with beasts;

and that the inefficient and occasionally benign rule of capitalism, which at least keeps the beasts in check, is a lesser evil. That proposition is Orwell's alpha and his omega.

So it is that the allegories of Soviet history in *Animal Farm* are just that—translations of the fall of Trotsky, the failure of the electrification program, the enforcement of collectivisation, of a ruling élite looking for scapegoats for its own errors or for other catastrophes. Nothing in the use of an animal society as the vehicle of allegory particularly illuminates or enhances it or the points it seeks to make. It certainly does not make the case against Soviet socialism any more convincing. In fact it appears to confirm the underlying hostility of its opponents to any suggestion that the working class can emancipate itself. It does nothing to cast light on what for any socialist is the real question: what has gone wrong and why? If anything it has tended to fix the left in its own errors by aversion.

Is this essay then a criticism of *Animal Farm* for what it is not, for lacking a stance which was never Orwell's anyway? It would be less than candid to deny that both its assumption that people and animals are alike in their social or political existence, and its use of that assumption to insult the belief that ordinary people can put an end to want and privilege, make *Animal Farm*, to this writer at least, a pretty unattractive book. But that is not what makes it a poor piece of literature.

## ANIMAL STORIES AS COMMENTATORS ON CLASS STRUCTURE

To take a second contrast from modern animal fiction, *The Wind in the Willows* is redolent of a particular social and political philosophy, all of it growing into and out of a beautifully told tale. Enough has been written about the class microcosm which contains the aristocratic playboy Toad, his yeoman friends Rat, Mole and Badger, and the feared (because unknown) Wild Wooders—the commoners, rogues and vagabonds. One can see and appraise Grahame's thoughts and feelings about class society and the stratum in which alone he feels secure, and one can have one's own views about them and him, without ever falling out with the fiction through which his idyll of contemplation and loyalty is conveyed.

The same is true of the misanthropy with which *Gulliver's Travels* is shot through. More to the point, both stories, because they work as stories, earn a measure of understanding for their authors' viewpoints. They enlarge intellectual as well as emotional horizons. . . .

Between its covers *Animal Farm* offers little that is creative, little that is original. Those who are interested in the links between politics and literature have far more to learn from the circumstances of the book's success. It is an extraordinary fact that it was written in the latter part of the Second World War, when the defeat of Nazism depended upon the Soviet Union's survival and military victory, and published (after three rejections) in the year of Labour's historic electoral victory. It was therefore certainly out of joint with its time, and it was no doubt in keeping with Orwell's penchant for heresy. But it was admirably in line with what rapidly became the political mode of government and press—a virulent and often unreasoning anti-communism. The prophet, to his own surprise, rapidly achieved honour in his own country.

When in 1947 Orwell wrote the preface to a Ukrainian edition of *Animal Farm* he explained that his aim had been to disabuse "the workers and intelligentsia in a country like England" of their naïve notions about the USSR (his Ukrainian readers were not there). He blamed their naïvety on the relative liberality of English political life:

> Yet one must remember that England is not completely democratic. It is also a capitalist country with great class privileges and (even now, after a war that has tended to equalise everybody) with great differences in wealth. But nevertheless it is a country in which people have lived together for several hundred years without knowing civil war, in which the laws are relatively just and official news and statistics can almost invariably be believed, and, last but not least, in which to hold and to voice minority views does not involve any mortal danger. In such an atmosphere the man in the street has no real understanding of things like concentration camps, mass deportations, arrests without trial, press censorship etc. Everything he reads about a country like the USSR is automatically translated into English terms, and he quite innocently accepts the lies of totalitarian propaganda.

This view of English political life in the mid-1940s does not now simply appear breathtakingly foolish; nor does it simply betray Orwell's socialism as a pose unsupported by analysis, experience or comprehension: it underscores *Animal Farm*'s message that ordinary people are too simpleminded to appreciate about Russia what is appreciated by a man who a page earlier has written:

> I have never visited Russia and my knowledge of it consists

only of what can be learned by reading books and newspapers.

He goes on in the preface to explain how, years after Spain, his thoughts were crystallised by seeing a small boy driving a huge cart-horse with a whip:

> It struck me that if only such animals became aware of their strength we should have no power over them, and that men exploit animals in much the same way as the rich exploit the proletariat.

> I proceeded to analyse Marx's theory from the animals' point of view. To them it was clear that the concept of a class struggle between humans was pure illusion, since whenever it was necessary to exploit animals, all humans united against them: the true struggle is between animals and humans. From this point of departure, it was not difficult to elaborate the story.

## MUDDLED THINKING

The muddle is remarkable. Where, for instance, does Marx argue that there is a class struggle between members of the ruling class ('a class struggle between humans')? More important, whether the idea that 'the true struggle is between animals and humans' is being attributed to the animals or to Orwell himself, the book begins and ends by debunking it, as of course it asks to be debunked. I have mentioned Major's fatuous early speech to this effect. The book goes on to argue that through revolution a human (that is a capitalist) oppressor will simply be replaced by an animal (that is a proletarian) oppressor. And remember how it ends?

> The creatures outside looked from pig to man, and from man to pig, and from pig to man again; but it was already impossible to say which was which.

If Orwell in his preface is trying to say simply that human beings, however divided among themselves, are united in their exploitation of animals, this is *not* the point of departure of *Animal Farm.* Its point of departure, like its conclusion, is the proposition that human beings and beasts share characteristics of greed and ruthlessness towards their own kind.

Orwell concluded his preface:

> I do not wish to comment on the work; if it does not speak for itself, it is a failure.

He was of course right: but it is an interesting comment on the ideological argument of *Animal Farm* that its author was so unable to give an intelligible account of it.

# The Fairy Tale Distances Us from the Terror

Patrick Reilly

Patrick Reilly is a scholar who has written a number
of literary studies, including one on Orwell and two
on Jonathan Swift, a satirist to whose work *Animal
Farm* is often compared. Reilly believes that George
Orwell very cleverly wrote *Animal Farm* in a comic
mode in order to expose in a palatable way the evils
of an idealistic revolution gone sour. In an unquoted
portion of the chapter from which the following
article was excerpted, Reilly points out the contrast
between *Animal Farm* and *1984*, which deal with
similar themes but in radically different ways. *1984*,
Orwell's last novel, is a powerful and much longer
examination of a society in which a dictator gains
absolute power over the citizens. It is the unrelent-
ingly bleak story of one man's abortive efforts to
"buck the system" in small ways—or even to survive
within the system. Although the hero, Winston
Smith, seems doomed, the novel successfully cap-
tures the reader's attention and emotions and has,
like *Animal Farm*, remained one of the best-read
novels of the twentieth century.

In *Animal Farm*, instead of taking the realistic approach
he favors in *1984*, Orwell follows the respectable tradition
of Jonathan Swift, whose rollicking satirical novel *Gulliver's Travels* pointed out follies of society in Swift's time.
Both writers knew that it is often easier to get people to listen if you entertain them rather than pound them over the
head with your message. Reilly suggests that both writers
were successful in achieving this aim.

Orwell will sacrifice art itself when life is in the other scale.
This is the core of his achievement, and a concern for life is

not so abundant, especially in our century, that we can afford to sniff at it. We, for our part, must ungrudgingly pay its price and not demand from the fervent truth-teller the cool detachment that a writer with more art and less mission might supply. "Aesthetic scrupulousness is not enough, but political rectitude is not enough either," Orwell wrote in one of his essays. In one book alone, as he himself recognised, did Orwell successfully integrate reformer and artist: "*Animal Farm* was the first book in which I tried, with full consciousness of what I was doing, to fuse political purpose and artistic purpose into one whole." In every other book we sense his active presence; here alone he realises Stephen Dedalus's ideal of the invisible creator and forsakes the easily detected ventriloquisms of earlier fictions. Ironically, it is the triumph of this disappearing-act that creates some of the most disconcerting problems for the reader.

The artistic triumph is inseparable from the chosen form; its good humour and equanimity stem from its status as animal fable. It was initially rejected by American publishers on the ground that there was no market for animal stories. We smile at a judgement so childishly blind to the allegorical import, yet this in itself is a tribute to the art. There is, in any case, something decisive about the Aesopian base: the choice of animals rather than human beings gave Orwell for the first time a certain latitude, release from that sense of moral constraint that otherwise held him captive, driving him to violate knowingly the unity of *Homage to Catalonia*, soliciting his own intervention throughout other books. The liberating secret lay in making animals behave like men.

## COMEDY VERGING ON NIGHTMARE

Men behaving like animals, if comic at all, makes for a comedy verging on nightmare, that of *Volpone* or *Gulliver's Travels*—the Yahoos alarm us not as beasts but as brothers, for Gulliver's shocking discovery is that beneath his European disguise he is a "perfect Yahoo." Animals behaving like men are, by contrast, inherently funny, the fact so assiduously exploited by Walt Disney—even the villainous tiger of *The Jungle Book* has proved irresistible to generations of delighted children. "Some fool has said that one cannot hate an animal; he should try a few nights in India, when the dogs are baying the moon," Orwell wrote in *Burmese Days*. The "fool" he rebukes is in fact right; *Animal Farm* is so exuberantly successful because one *cannot* hate an animal, not even when the animal is Napoleon, a nasty pig who is farmyard stand-in for a monstrous dictator.

The very style of the fable tames catastrophe through levity, resolves terror in comedy. In life Orwell dreaded totalitarian propaganda as the supreme iniquity of our time, the throttling of truth even as a theoretic possibility; in the art of *Animal Farm* the image of a pig up a ladder with a paintbrush alchemises the horror into humour, putting Orwell and the reader in serene control of the situation. If the other animals are taken in by Squealer's impudent trickery, so much the worse for them—the reader isn't such a fool, and when he laughs at the bungled cheat he simultaneously proclaims his happy superiority to it. Material unbearable in life becomes in art a source of comic delight. When the newly liberated animals, obedient to the first duties of the victors, bring out the hams from Jones's kitchen to enact the solemn ritual of interment, the reader is invited to smile rather than mourn.

## COMEDY RULES

In a book where comedy rules, it is fitting that Jones should be chased off the farm with no more than a few butts and kicks, that, after his pride, his backside is the most serious casualty of the Battle of the Cowshed. Admittedly, his eventual death in alcoholic delirium is horrific enough, but it is self-inflicted, and, like the catastrophes of classical drama, occurs off-stage. The fable is inhospitable to anything resembling the ghastly conclusion in the cellar at Ekaterinburg [where the last Russian Czar and his family were murdered]—the reader would be revolted at the Joneses trampled to death under the horses' hooves or devoured by the dogs. We only hear that Jones has children because of the old discarded spelling-book which the pigs rescue from the rubbish heap in order to learn to read. In fact the Czar's children, not their primer, were flung on the rubbish heap, but the fable softens reality. Orwell insists on a victimless revolution. When, later, the men invade the farm, Orwell will not allow any of them to be killed in the successful counterattack. Boxer's massive hoof catches a stable lad on the skull, leaving him apparently "stretched . . . lifeless in the mud." But here too there is the same welcome reassurance as in Shakespeare's play *The Tempest*: "Tell your piteous heart / There's no harm done."

Boxer's solicitude is upheld against Snowball's ferocity. Pawing grief-stricken at the inert body, Boxer is rebuked by the pig for his sentimentality: "War is war. The only good human being is a dead one." Orwell knows how insidiously easy it is to become infected with war fever: "I do think it is a dreadful effect of war that one is actually pleased to hear of an enemy sub going to the bottom," he wrote in an essay. He feared the temptation of vindictiveness the more because he had experienced the emotion in himself: "That bastard Chiappe is cold meat. Everyone delighted, as when Balbo died. This war is at any rate killing off a few Fascists." From this, if unchecked, it is a straight descent to the cinema audience of *Nineteen Eighty-Four* enjoying the newsreels of "enemy" women and children being strafed by planes from Airstrip One. But Boxer in the audience would not be rejoicing. Even human life is precious to him; he has no enemies that he wants dead—his human equivalent will not be found administering the Gulag or Auschwitz—and, Snowball's jungle realism notwithstanding, his eyes are full of tears. Orwell plainly sides with the horse.

In any case, Snowball is wrong, factually as well as morally: this is *not* war, but is limited, at Orwell's insistence, to cuts and bruises. The animals leave to search for the missing Mollie and when they return the stable lad has scampered—he has merely been stunned: "the child is not dead but sleepeth." Orwell vetoes extreme violence, whether by men against animals or animals against men; when, finally, it does erupt, it is ironically inflicted by animals upon animals, not because Orwell wishes it so, but because this is the tragedy which even the comic fable cannot conceal.

Nevertheless, it is crucially decisive that the tragedy happens to and among animals. The reader *knows* everything in *Animal Farm*—it is the animals who are forever mystified right up to the final bewildering metamorphosis. . . .

## READER IS IN CONTROL

In *Animal Farm,* apart from a possible irritation at being forced to choose between Napoleon and Boxer (the available options within the text are unacceptable, while the acceptable option is not available), the reader is always in control of the fable. The villain of *Animal Farm,* unlike those of *Othello* or *Nineteen Eighty-Four,* is always pellucidly open, often derisively so—we never *fear* Napoleon as we do Iago and Big Brother. The reader is in the superior position of a sophisticated onlooker at a country fair watching a bunch of yokels being taken in by a third-rate charlatan. Orwell castrates terror in the comic spectacle of an allegedly teetotal pig suffering from a hangover and swearing, like the rest of us, never to do it again. It is a scene not from the world of totalitarian terror, of Hitler and Stalin, purges and camps, but from that of Donald McGill [a British comic] of mothers-in-law, dirty weekends and marital squabbles.

Naturally, the animals take a very different view of things, but the reader sees Napoleon less as a ferocious tyrant than as a comic cheat whose inept attempts at duplicity provoke laughter rather than indignation. When human tyrants suffer hangovers, they presumably become more fearful as the executions mount with the migraines. In Orwell's *Nineteen Eighty-Four*, we are forced to identify with Winston, the main character, and we fear Big Brother, and rightly, for our lives hang upon his whims. In *Nineteen Eighty-Four* the reader is included *in* the diminishing-technique, which makes him an insignificant bug like Winston, liable at any instant to be squashed into unpersonhood. In *Animal Farm*, by contrast, the reader is serenely above the diminution, watching with amused immunity the terrifying tale of contemporary history scaled to Lilliputian proportions, tamed to the level of barnyard fable. The prophecy magnifies the tyrant and diminishes the reader; the allegory magnifies the reader and diminishes the tyrant.

Orwell knew from personal experience how thoroughly dislikable pigs could be: He wrote in a letter: "The pig has grown to a stupendous size and goes to the butcher next week. We are all longing to get rid of him, as he is so destructive and greedy, even gets into the kitchen at times." In life the troublesome pig goes to the butcher; in the nightmare fairy tale the pig decides who goes to the butcher and is not just occasionally in the kitchen but in unchallengeable control of the house itself. But the trivialisation implicit in the fable form necessarily keeps the reader superior and secure.

All the evens are deliberately diminished. The suppression of the kulaks in the Ukraine is reduced to a rebellion of hens at the sale of their eggs; it ends with nine hens starved to death—the fable's equivalent of the millions of peasants who died in the aftermath of Stalin's victory. Swift in Lilliput similarly trivialises the wars of the Reformation to an absurd wrangle between Big- and Little-Endians. Orwell employs the same technique to exchange the harrowing emotions provoked by twentieth-century history for an Olympian pose, so making the events easier to handle. The allegations of industrial sabotage which issued in the Moscow showcase trials dwindle into a broken window and a blocked drain, while treason to the Revolution finds its appropriate image in a sheep urinating in a drinking-pool.

The most amusingly "domestic" of these substitutions is the account of Mollie's defection. We hear that she is becoming "more and more troublesome," and there are rumors of "something more serious" than her habitual giddiness. What Marxist and social philosopher Herbert Marcuse deplores as the seduction of large sections of the Western working class, bribed by the titbits of consumerism, is here depicted in terms of a fallen woman of Victorian melodrama, as Mollie goes down the well-worn road of Little Em'ly and Hetty Sorrel. The matronly Clover does her best to save the wanton—she is accepting sugar and ribbons from the men, has even been caught *in flagrante delicto* allowing her nose to be stroked—but the attempted rescue is as futile as Mrs Poyser's remonstrations. The last the scandalised animals hear is that Mollie is traipsing about town with a vulgar publican; after this, "none of the animals ever mentioned Mollie again." The shame of the lapse is emphasized in the best Victorian tradition. When the animals metaphorically turn Mollie's face to the wall, the reader applauds the reductive wit, and, in his amusement, necessarily neglects the seriousness of the defection as viewed from Marcuse's perspective. . . .

Orwell's purpose is to control a material which, taken at its everyday estimate and customary magnification, would cause the writer pain, alarm and indignation. Small is masterable; when Stalin becomes a pig and Europe a farmyard, the nightmare of contemporary history is transmuted, through the power of art, into a blithe and inspired fantasy.

Thus to criticise Orwell for allegedly demeaning the common people by depicting them as moronically credulous brutes is to misread the book. The animal fable is devised not to insult the ordinary man but to distance Orwell from the terror: existence becomes endurable as an aesthetic phenomenon. Philosopher Schiller argues that only in art is man free. German novelist Thomas Mann described his Joseph tetralogy [a series of books], written between 1926 and 1943 (the period covered by Orwell's fable), as his attempt to escape the horror by burying himself in an innocent and serene creation of the Spirit. Simplicity is an essential part of Orwell's disarming strategy. *Animal Farm*, as its subtitle "A Fairy Tale" makes plain, is a convenient simplification, yet its simplicity came hard: "the only one of my books I really sweated over," he wrote. Orwell's efforts were fully justified. . . .

## COMIC CONTROL

The decision establishes the style of comic control, which Orwell only occasionally deserts to inject a more exalted, more sombre, sometimes more chilling note into the tale. His own unquestionable commitment to the revolutionary ideal is reflected in the elevated style with which he describes the morning after liberation and the sentiments of the triumphant animals. As they survey the familiar landscape in "the clear morning light" of the new dispensation's first dawn, existence suddenly becomes a festival newly appreciated: "it was as though they had never seen these things before." Behold, I make all things new. The fun is momentarily forgotten in the high emotional contagion of the revolutionary hope.

Nor is there any fun, though for a very different reason, in the description of the stunned reaction to Snowball's flight from Napoleon's dogs: "silent and terrified, the animals crept back into the barn." All the levity vanishes with the vanished Snowball, yet even this incident is merely a rehearsal for the climactic horror of the purges. As soon as the accused pigs confess, "the dogs promptly tore their throats out"—the fate which Jones is not allowed to suffer. The bloodletting continues: Hens, pigs, sheep "were all slain on the spot. And so the tale of confessions and executions went on, until there was a pile of corpses lying before Napoleon's feet and the air was heavy with the smell of blood, which had been unknown there since the expulsion of Jones." No longer can the reader smile, for the weight of that blood-impregnated air presses heavy upon him too, as Napoleon becomes Mooch. The mood here is much closer to the Miniluv chapters of *Nineteen Eighty-Four* than to the Aesopian fable that has hitherto charmed us.

Hard upon the scene of blood comes the pastoral scene when the stricken animals retreat into the beauty of the landscape to reprieve their shattered spirits. Yet this very beauty has taken on a plangent heartbreaking quality: "as Clover looked upon the hillside her eyes filled with tears." The serene landscape and the high utopian aspirations consort so ill with the recent carnage that all Clover can do is weep, while Boxer hauls stones to stupefy himself.

At the opening of the final chapter Orwell employs yet another style to evoke a mood of elegaic intensity: "years passed. The seasons came and went, the short animal lives fled by. A time came when there was no one who remembered the old days before the Rebellion. . . . Muriel was dead; Bluebell, Jessie and Pincher were dead . . . ." It is the same melancholic chord that sounds through Matthew Arnold's famous poem "Dover Beach," bringing "the eternal note of sadness in"; and it is a tribute to the flexibility of Orwell's style that the book can accommodate such diverse moods, be hospitable to comedy, pathos and satire without pulling itself apart.

Nevertheless, joy is the paramount emotion of the book, and the delight of the creative imagination in so triumphantly alchemising the sordid material which are its datum—we have art, says Nietzsche, that we may not perish of the truth—is irrepressibly there from the opening paragraph when the drunken farmer lurches to bed, "with the ring of light from his lantern dancing from side to side." No sooner is his bedroom light extinguished than the farm leaps to life, with a "stirring" and a "fluttering" all through its animal quarters. While the humans snore in heedless, intoxicated irresponsibility, the animal world is vibrantly awake, and the book mimics the lantern in the dance which it initiates and sustains; the book dances with the lantern, is a dancing-book as no other book of Orwell's is. . . .

The great experiment must, of course, begin in elation because its end is disillusion. Yet Old Major's dream of the elusively just society, submit though it must to the scrutiny of reason and the probings of scepticism, is not one that the book commends us to discard as worthless or obsolete. To settle for the world's injustice as ineluctably given, a datum of existence at which only fools will cavil, ranges one compromisingly with the knaves who urge the "wisdom" of acceptance to justify their own depravities. Orwell himself never ceased to dream, however guardedly and with prophylactic self-derision, of the just society which he had seen flower briefly in Barcelona [during the Spanish Civil War].

# CHAPTER 3

# *Animal Farm* as Sociopolitical Commentary

# Mealymouthed Critics Ignore *Animal Farm's* Anticommunist Flavor

Spencer Brown

From 1950 to 1954 the United States suffered an extreme episode of anticommunist paranoia. Wisconsin senator Joseph McCarthy struck a strong note in the hearts of Americans who had become disillusioned with and wary of their former ally, Soviet Russia. McCarthy's virulent movement to demonize the political left and, specifically, communism was sparked by his 1950 speech in Wheeling, West Virginia, in which he asserted that he had a list of "card-carrying members of the Communist Party" who were employed by the U.S. Department of State. In a country that had already become suspicious of Russia, this was like a bombshell. With the aid of McCarthy and his Senate hearings, accusations were made against high-level politicians, entertainers, military personnel, writers, professors, and all manner of people, few of whom could withstand the furor of public opinion. Even though McCarthy's fall began in 1954 when he was accused of financial improprieties, the impact of those paranoid days were long felt. It was decades before some of the people blacklisted during the McCarthy era were able to work in their chosen professions again.

No wonder, then, that in 1955, when the following viewpoint was written, people were wary of being called either a communist or a McCarthyite. Nevertheless, Spencer Brown, the author of this viewpoint, argues that commentators on *Animal Farm* were going out of their way to avoid the truth of what Orwell was writing about: the evils of communism. Brown, who teaches history at Western Illinois University, states that *Animal Farm* is the best anticommunist novel ever written, yet critics persist in discussing it as though it has nothing in particular to do with Russia; as though it is a generic antitotalitarianism book. Spencer points out the book's strong parallels with Russian history and asserts that these were not accidental; Orwell wanted to show the evils of the Russian government. Spencer suggests that critics who ignored the Russian issue did so out of fear of being compared to Joseph McCarthy. This was both cowardly and hypocritical, he states.

Published in 1946, George Orwell's *Animal Farm* remains to this day, in my opinion, the best of anti-Communist books. If we had to do without all the others, fine as some of them are—Koestler, Dallin, Silone, Borkenau, Serge, and the rest—and were left with Orwell alone, we could still get by. For no other writer has shown us so clearly the worst tragedy of our age, worse in one respect at least than the crimes of the Nazis, for the Soviet tyranny combines with its terror the utter perversion of man's highest ideals.

The story is a detailed parallel with the Russian Revolution and its aftermath, from 1917 to 1945. The drunken farmer Jones flees from his mistreated and aroused animals, who, following the teachings of the late boar Major, set up an egalitarian commonwealth and attempt to run the farm by and for themselves. Few of them, unfortunately, are intelligent enough to do anything but heavy labor, and the direction of things gradually devolves upon the pigs, who lead a successful defense against Jones's armed intervention. A struggle for power develops between the two leading pigs, Napoleon (Stalin) and Snowball (Trotsky). Napoleon, by means of his Chekist (GPU, NKVD, MVD) dogs, exiles Snowball, seizes absolute power, and sets about building a windmill (the Dnieper Dam, symbol of Russia's industrialization) originally planned by Snowball.

The hardest work is done by the horse Boxer, who represents the long suffering, toiling, loyal Russian people. Because of faulty construction, the windmill collapses and, when rebuilt, is again destroyed by a neighboring farmer, Frederick (Hitler), who attacks Animal Farm shortly after swindling Napoleon in a timber deal. Frederick's men are at last routed, at terrible cost. Wounded in the war but still working to rebuild the mill, the superannuated Boxer is sent to the Knacker's to be boiled down for glue. Napoleon has by this time revised all the egalitarian principles of Animalism, originally enunciated by Major and codified by Snowball, to read: "All animals are equal but some animals are more equal than others." Having assumed human vices, Napoleon gives a banquet for another neighbor, Pilkington (the English ruling classes), at which they drink each other's health colossally and cheat each other in a card game. The bewildered animal slaves, watching from outside the windows, can no longer tell which is man and which is pig.

## PARALLELS TO THE RUSSIAN REVOLUTION

The parallels with the Russian Revolution are three and four to the page. Indeed, some critics wholly friendly to Orwell and his anti-Communism find this plain, point-by-point historical correspondence an artistic defect. I cannot agree. I find *Animal Farm* a *tour de force*, but one of such extraordinary ease and realism in every phrase and incident that it is a masterpiece apart from the satire, and also a masterpiece of satire in which moral purity and breadth of human sympathy are combined with crushing wit.

At the center of *Animal Farm* is Orwell's sadness, and our sadness, as the hope of our century transforms itself before our eyes into total evil:

> Never had the farm—and with a kind of surprise they remembered that it was their own farm, every inch of it their own property—appeared to the animals so desirable a place. As Clover looked down the hillside her eyes filled with tears. If she could have spoken her thoughts, it would have been to say that this was not what they had aimed at when they set themselves years ago to work for the overthrow of the human race. These scenes of terror and slaughter were not what they had looked forward to on that night when old Major first stirred them to rebellion. If she herself had had any picture of the future, it had been of a society of animals set free from hunger and the whip, all equal, each working according to his capacity, the strong protecting the weak, as she had protected the lost brood of ducklings with her foreleg on the night of Major's speech. Instead—she did not know why— they had come to a time when no one dared speak his mind, when fierce, growling dogs roamed everywhere, and when you had to watch your comrades torn to pieces after confessing shocking crimes.

This is George Orwell at his best, and our century at its best. Being unable to make a wreath of my own, I lay his wreath on his grave.

Now *Animal Farm* has been made into a full-length cartoon film by the English husband-and-wife team of John Halas and Joy Batchelor. Released by Louis de Rochemont Associates, it opened at the Paris Theater in New York on December 29. And thereby hangs more of a tale than the hopes and disappointments of animals.

Much of the satire of Orwell's novel—or for that matter of such similar works as *Gulliver's Travels* and *Penguin Island*—

### ATTACK ON CAPITALISM

Animal Farm *is widely known as an attack on Russian communism. However, critic Richard Voorhees points out in* The Paradox of George Orwell, *that does not mean that Orwell was supporting capitalism. Quite the contrary.*

Although an attack on totalitarianism, *Animal Farm* is a long way from being a defense of capitalism, British or otherwise. Of course, Orwell is shooting mainly at the Russian Revolution and its results, but he also fires some shots at reactions in other countries to the events in Russia. When the animals first get control of the farm, the people of the countryside predict that they will not be able to run it and will therefore starve. Then, when it is clear that the beasts are not starving, the people circulate rumors about the terrible wickedness of the new establishment: the animals torture one another with red-hot horseshoes, have their females in common, and practice cannibalism. When the anthem of Animal Farm, "The Beasts of England," becomes popular on other farms as well, the human beings are infuriated and frightened, but they pretend to think that the song is altogether absurd. They cannot understand, they say, "how even animals could bring themselves to sing such contemptible rubbish." In the last few pages of the book Orwell attacks the capitalist from another angle. The pigs, after replacing the tyranny of Farmer Jones with their own, give a dinner for some neighboring farmers, one of whom explains in a two-page speech that they can get along in jolly fashion because they have, after all, the same objectives. He winds up his speech with a joke which sets the table aroar: "If you have your lower animals to contend with, we have our lower classes." The early history of Animal Farm, then, is partly a satire of the Tory protesting against any form of social change because he fears and hates it; the later history is partly a satire of the Tory wanting to get along well with dictatorships because it is good business to do so.

must remain inaccessible to this or any film. The wry, laconic understatement, the backlash of wit, can be selected from but not rendered entire, for the pace of the motion picture is incomparably slower than that of prose fiction. Nevertheless the film has many merits, stemming chiefly from Orwell's ingenuity in incident and his marvelous knack of securing the suspension of disbelief by sympathetic and detailed realism.

It has certain defects, too, worst among which is the animators' revision of the ending: the sorrow of Orwell's animals is unrelieved, intensified finally by the realization that their revolution and suffering have been in vain, that their pig-exploiters are no different, even in appearance, from Mr. Pilkington. In the Halas-Batchelor film, however, it is not human exploiters who attend Napoleon's orgy, but other pig-bureaucrats from pig satrapies elsewhere. They all get drunk, the animals of the world unite in revolt and converge on Animal Farm, Napoleon whistles to his dogs for help, but they too are sodden in liquor and unable to prevent the overthrow of the tyrant. 'Tis the final conflict—a truly Trotskyite touch, but notably out of keeping with Orwell's melancholy view of world politics.

Another detail that might be objected to is the excessive prettying up of the animals' toil. When they are getting in the harvest and when Boxer prances as he pulls stone for the windmill, one almost expects the Seven Dwarfs to pop round the barn, singing "Hi-Ho" and pitching in with right good will. The temptation to Disneyize must have been irresistible, but Disney is not Orwell.

Yet with its flaws, the film has not seriously damaged Orwell and may have the merit of bringing his satire to those who do not know the novel. In the promotion of the film, however, and in the response of the critics, something happened that is worthy of note.

## Mealymouthed Marketers

What, according to critics and advertisers, is Orwell's anti-Communist classic *Animal Farm*?

It is, says Bosley Crowther in the New York *Times*, "a pretty brutal demonstration of the vicious cycle of tyranny"; it presents "the leaders of the new Power State as pigs" and conveys "a sense of the monstrous hypocrisy of the totalitarian leader type." In a lengthy review, Mr. Crowther never comes closer than this to mentioning Russia.

It is, says Otis L. Guernsey, Jr., in the *Herald Tribune*, "a political parable satirizing the various isms in a story about animals taking over a farm and founding their own society.... It tells how an animals' revolution is converted into a pigs' Fascism with the passage of time and the corruption of democratic ideals."

"The main point about *Animal Farm*," says Archer Winsten in the New York *Post*, "is that it has something to say about dictatorships, democracy, and the conflicts between those who toil and those who rule. It says this without pulling punches." It is "intelligence week" at the Paris Theater, says Mr. Winsten, providing "egghead ecstasy." For the program also includes an old March of Time [newsreel] on Huey Long and is "of extraordinary, inter-related quality."...

Even in the *Daily News*, where one might expect something else, Wanda Hale writes, truly but vaguely: "Like Orwell's fable, the film is a vitriolic satire on dictatorship, uncomfortably realistic in the comparison of man to the lower form of animal and a frightening example of the oppressed masses under tyrannical rulers drunk with power." She does not mention Russia.

In the *Herald Tribune*'s advance story on the making of the film, we learn that "In *Animal Farm* Orwell was satirizing the Dictator State in terms of Animals vs. Man.... The parable follows close to the history of twentieth-century totalitarianism."

As late as January 16, Mr. Crowther wrote in the Sunday *Times*: "These two highly facile young artists have converted the Orwell parody of a totalitarian political system into a clever and sardonic cartoon that is touched with bits of tearful pathos and barbed with trenchant points of caricature...."

Still no word about Russia.

The promotion of the film had been in the same general vein. In a publicity handout before the opening, Irving Drutman, of Louis de Rochemont Associates, says: "Orwell's world-renowned satirical fable, which lampoons the modern Power State, deals with the revolt against the tyrannical Farmer Brown [*sic*].... The parable ironically parallels the history of the 20th century."...

## TRUTH OF THE SATIRE IS WHITEWASHED

All this is embarrassing to me, since as a teacher I have for some years been recommending *Animal Farm* to my students. Frequently one of them reports in class on the novel, usually with enthusiasm, for the story of the animals who in their inept innocence try to solve problems that the human race has failed to solve is both humorously and deeply pathetic. All the students except those completely ignorant of modern history recognize that the story parallels the Russian Revolution. Without assistance they identify Napoleon as Stalin, Jones as the Czar, and Frederick as Hitler; if they have ever heard of Trotsky, they recognize him at once as Snowball. Other niceties of Orwell's satire, such as the changes of line, the ban on singing the "Internationale," the rewritings of history, are spotted only by the sophisticated. In all these years, no student has yet come up with the notion that the fable is about either the Nazis or Senator McCarthy (of whom they *have* heard).

Fortunately, if any of my students should ever reproach me for having misled them on the meaning of *Animal Farm*, there will be one or two authorities to whom I can appeal. Delmore Schwartz, in the *New Republic*, does say quite clearly that *Animal Farm* is about Russia, though he thinks the film frequently clumsy and generally unsatisfactory. *Time*'s reviewer, too, had by January 17 either heard what was happening or figured the thing out for himself, for he discusses "George Orwell's political fable, the famous animallegory about Communism." Rose Pelswick, in the *Journal-American* of December 30, begins her review with: "Based on the powerful anti-Communist fable of George Orwell, the picture is an interesting adaptation. . . ." And Alton Cook, in the *World-Telegram and Sun*, says: "If you were attentive to your homework on the book pages back in 1946, you will recall that the novel was a biting satire on the rise of the Communist dictatorship. Animals revolted against their farmer owner and events paralleled the course of the Russian Revolution." Mr. Cook concludes: "The Communists never had it so rough."

It is interesting that three out of these four reviews appeared in "right-wing" publications. Has truth become a luxury no longer available to liberals? . . .

A middle course was taken when it came to Louis Berg, of *This Week*. Back in August 1953, Mr. Berg wrote a piece on *Animal Farm*. It was illustrated with drawings from the film-in-progress, including a marvelous sketch (unfortunately omitted from the finished film) of the Politburo Pigs on the reviewing stand watching their animal slaves march past. Mr. Berg called *Animal Farm* a "devastating satire on Russian Communism," and commended the forthcoming film as a faithful adaptation of the book. Mr. Berg's piece was called "The Fable That Rocked the Kremlin." But the early ads for the film, for example in the *Times* for December 31, read: "'A devastating satire—an important film!' (Berg, *This Week* Magazine)."

---

**DISTORTING ORWELL**

*In the March 1955 issue of* Commentary, *Albert Margolies asserts that critics betray themselves and their readers when they refuse to honestly describe* Animal Farm *as an anticommunist novel.*

Why, then, have [critics], each of them a serious student of the cinema, seen fit, all on their own, to distort George Orwell during the brief journey from the screen to their typewriters? Why have they so unconscionably undertaken to mislead their readers into believing that Orwell wrote about some anonymous "Power State" and not about Russia; about a dictator and not about Stalin; about a secret police and not about the NKVD; about totalitarianism and not Communism? Why did they ignore the anti-Soviet point in the Orwell film? . . .

To have called *Animal Farm* an anti-Communist, anti-Soviet film would have been to tell the truth about it. But the Crowthers, the Guernseys, the Winstens and the others apparently believe that it is better to be "progressive" than accurate. Let's not red-bait, I can imagine them telling themselves, for red-baiting is "McCarthyism." And they sat down and wrote what they did without stopping to consider how they might be helping to shield the Soviet Union.

Both the Communists and McCarthy have reason to be satisfied. As they regard the timidity and the fears of the intelligentsia, they know that they are the happy parents of a big bouncing baby monster.

---

As a matter of fact, the publication and advertising history of the novel *Animal Farm* in this country might have prepared us for the kind of promotion by selective quotation that has been given to the film.

Before its acceptance by Harcourt, Brace and Company, *Animal Farm* was turned down by eighteen or twenty American publishers—notable among them Little, Brown and

Company, whose then editor, Angus Cameron, wielded his hatchet on many an anti-Communist book while pushing Howard Fast and Albert E. Kahn. (Equally notable, perhaps, is the publisher who turned it down because "there's no market for animal stories.") When Harcourt, Brace at last published the book, the advertising material on the dust-jacket did not mention Russia or Communism, but proclaimed, instead: "About this little book there is the same kind of reality one concedes to *Alice in Wonderland.*" The author of that sentence is like Homer in one way—in being unable to read.

Of course, one might say, that was in 1946 when we were still in the afterglow of the wartime alliance with Russia and there might still have been a Communist under a bed here and there. However, as it happened, even at that time some of the literary critics were not so nervous as the publishers. *Animal Farm* was a Book of the Month Club selection in August 1946. Harry Scherman, president of the Club, made an almost unprecedented appeal to members not to make use of their substitution privilege that month, and commended to their attention the review by Christopher Morley in the same issue of the Club's *News.* Mr. Morley's review begins: "In a narrative so plain that a child will enjoy it, yet with double meanings as cruel and comic as any great cartoon, George Orwell presents a parable that may rank as one of the great political satires of our anxious time. . . . It is plain enough that the satire is explicitly turned on Russian Communism, yet I also wish that the reader might see in it a parable even larger than that."

The point was made more fully by Arthur M. Schlesinger, Jr., who in the *Times* book section for August 25, 1946, concluded his acute and admiring review thus: "Appreciation of the precision and bite of the satire increases with knowledge of the events in Russia. The steadiness and lucidity of Orwell's merciless wit are reminiscent of Anatole France and even of Swift. The exact and deadpan transposition of the struggle between Stalin and Trotsky, the fight over industrialization, the Moscow trials, the diplomatic shenanigans with Britain and Germany, the NKVD, the resurrection of the state church, and so on, will be a continuing delight to anyone familiar with recent Soviet developments. The story should be read in particular by liberals who still cannot understand how Soviet performance has fallen so far behind

Communist professions. *Animal Farm* is a wise, compassionate and illuminating fable for our times."

Now it is 1955, when all America has had the disillusioning lessons of ten years of postwar experience with the Soviet rulers, and when domestic Communist influence, we understand, no longer exists. So how account for the fact that, when Harcourt, Brace now decides to reissue *Animal Farm* to accompany the film, Mr. Morley and Mr. Schlesinger are quoted on the dust-jacket in curiously adapted versions? On the front cover is the quotation from Christopher Morley: "A parable that may rank as one of the great political satires of our anxious time." Inside the cover is a long quotation from Mr. Scherman, fortunately innocuous but demonstrating that space was not lacking, and the same quotation from Mr. Morley. Then this from Mr. Schlesinger: "A wise, compassionate and illuminating fable for our times.... The steadiness and lucidity of Orwell's merciless wit are reminiscent of Anatole France and even of Swift."

This, too, has some of the "reality one concedes *to Alice in Wonderland*."

## UNMENTIONING RUSSIA

Am I only trying to stir up a tempest in a samovar? After all, you may ask, what's the harm if the critics see *Animal Farm* as a "universal" satire on all tyrannies everywhere? Anyway, isn't it obvious that the satire applies to Russia? Why labor the obvious?

Well, it is not, as it happens, a "universal" satire. No doubt *Animal Farm* has "universal" implications. So does Swift's *A Modest Proposal*. But *A Modest Proposal* is about British oppression of the Irish peasantry, and *Animal Farm* is about the Bolshevik betrayal of the people of Russia. Do we add to our sense of the "universal" by omitting these facts? If so, then perhaps we might enrich our sense of American history by forgetting the issues involved in the Civil War, omitting the names of Abraham Lincoln and Jefferson Davis, and remembering only that the war was an example of the eternal aggressiveness of the human spirit.

Can the parable of *Animal Farm* be applied equally to all forms of totalitarianism? My "reinterpretation" of this fable as it would apply to Nazi Germany should, I think, stand as a sufficient answer. Those who unmention Russia are asking us to believe that so sophisticated an anti-Communist as

George Orwell wrote a book in which *by mere accident* every event and every character can be shown to correspond *exactly* to some fact, general or particular, of Soviet history. Moreover, it is clear that the demagogy in *Animal Farm* can only be the demagogy of a dictatorship whose origin was egalitarian and pacifist socialism: *Comrade* Napoleon— when was it ever *Comrade* Hitler or *Comrade* Mussolini? The Nazis and Fascists specifically condemned equality and socialism and denounced democracy as corrupt. Only the Communists claimed to be more democratic than anyone else; only to the Communists could one satirically attribute such a slogan as "All animals are equal but some animals are more equal than others."

As for laboring the obvious: in reviewing a film about Sister Kenny, for example, would critics avoid using the word "polio"? Would they refer instead to "a controversial disease"? Would they find "a clear and unmistakable reference to a scientific problem of interest to every patient and doctor"? Would they commend the film, in spite of defects, as "having something to say about medicine, suffering, and therapy"? Would they fail to mention Sister Kenny by name, and make only elliptical references that might apply as well to Koch or Pasteur? Or, politically speaking, when Chaplin made *The Great Dictator,* did these critics fail to indicate, by outright statement and unambiguous leer, that the butt of Chaplin's satire was Hitler?

Perhaps it is worth mentioning that the Communists themselves seem to know very well what the book is about. Mr. David Platt, in the Sunday *Worker* of January 9, writes: "This list would not be complete without a mention of Louis de Rochemont's feature-length cartoon based on George Orwell's anti-human novel 'Animal Farm' which was intended to frighten people out of any belief in the possibility of social progress. The point of the cartoon was that the overthrow of capitalism can bring only ruin to the world, that a society based on the people's rule carries within it the seeds of its eventual destruction." Mr. Platt, obviously, is not a liberal, and he has given the game away: *Animal Farm is* an attack on Russian Communism.

### ADVERTISING TURNAROUND

This, however, is not quite the end of our story of the liberal mind's visit to *Animal Farm.* About two weeks after the picture opened, a change took place, not suddenly but yet with fair rapidity. On January 7, there appeared in the ads a quotation from Mr. Cook (but an innocuous one); and Mr. Berg's phrase, "The Fable That Rocked the Kremlin," not only appeared but headed the list of endorsements. And there are other signs that from now on the film will be presented and advertised for what it is—a fable about Russian Communism. On January 16, the ad for the film in the Sunday *Times* was a reprint from the review in *Time.* Apparently someone has discovered that the fable isn't really so "universal" after all.

How was that discovery made? And why did it take so long to make it? Why do people spend three years of painstaking labor on an anti-Communist film only to deny, when the job is finished, that it *is* anti-Communist? I have no answers to these questions. Advertising is a mysterious business, and liberalism these days seems to be a mysterious business too; when you put the two mysteries together, you get something like the kind of story I have been telling. Perhaps Mr. Crowther, Mr. Guernsey, Mr. Winsten, et al., and Mr. de Rochemont and his associates, might help to clarify what happened and why.

I think the whole story would tickle George Orwell's satiric sense, though no doubt it would also depress him to see how long some people have taken to learn so little.

# Orwell Shows That Too Much Civilizing Can Harm Good Instincts

David L. Kubal

George Orwell is often said to have loved animals. He grew up around them and often wrote about them. David L. Kubal, a college English teacher, says that Orwell viewed animals as "communal, loyal, and self-sacrificing." Certainly, that is the way Orwell portrays them at the beginning of *Animal Farm*. They survive together against the terrible tyranny of Farmer Jones, and once they decide to rebel, they do it together, vowing that they will all be equal in the new, farmerless society they will form. After their rebellion succeeds, however, some of the animals begin to become more "civilized"—they wear human garments and eventually walk on two legs as humans do. They also begin to tyrannize their fellows. Kubal says that Orwell uses this example to show how humans can similarly become too "civilized" and forget the ties that bind them to their fellow humans, allowing them, too, to tyrannize their former comrades.

Throughout his life, Orwell had a deep affection for animals. Although he often criticized the English for showing coddling devotion to dogs and cats, he frequently wrote of animals with feeling and in the same way as D.H. Lawrence was able to empathize with them. In general he admired their ability to endure human tyranny as well as their faithfulness. In "Marrakech" he describes the Moroccan donkey:

> hardly bigger than a St Bernard dog, it carries a load which in the British Army would be considered too much for a fifteen-hands mule, and very often its pack-saddle is not taken off its back for weeks together. But what is peculiarly

From *Outside the Whale: George Orwell's Art and Politics* by David L. Kubal; ©1972 by the University of Notre Dame Press, Notre Dame, Indiana. Reprinted by permission of the publisher.

pitiful is that it is the most willing creature on earth, it follows its master like a dog and does not need either bridle or halter. After a dozen years of devoted work it suddenly drops dead, whereupon its master tips it into the ditch and the village dogs have torn its guts out before it is cold.

He also saw in the animal realm the facility for surviving nature itself. For example, he was reassured in the spring not only by the appearance of birds, but also by the resurrection of the common toad. It gave him a special kind of pleasure to know even the ugly and unappealing could come through.

In the truest sense Orwell was a man of reverence. He venerated nature not in a shallow, romantic way, nor finally because of an attachment to preindustrial culture; rather he approached it as sacred and sacramental. Like Thomas Hardy and—again—Lawrence, he viewed any attack on nature as a denial of the sanctity of life; man's brutality toward animals, for instance, signified for him an outright negation of existence. Elizabeth Lackersteen's pleasure in killing the Imperial pigeons, analogous to Gerald Crich's subjugation of the mare in *Women in Love*, reflects a hatred of self and the world. On the other side, George Bowling's attitude toward fish indicates his vital connection with life. Domestic animals, we recall, are eliminated in Oceania [in Orwell's novel *1984*].

## IN AWE OF THE STRUGGLE FOR EXISTENCE

In the last analysis, however, Orwell was awed by both animate and inanimate nature for the same reason he revered the human person. In all being he saw and rejoiced in the desperate struggle for existence against insuperable odds. He did not overlook the impulse toward death in creation; he accepted it. Yet he stressed its opposite and, like Freud, saw the instinct to survive as possessing cultural value. He would have agreed, I think, with Lionel Trilling [who wrote] that Freud's emphasis on biology represents

> a resistance to and a modification of the cultural omnipotence. We reflect that somewhere in the child, somewhere in the adult, there is a hard, irreducible, stubborn core of biological urgency, and biological necessity, and biological *reason*, that culture cannot reach and that reserves the right, which sooner or later it will exercise, to judge the culture and resist and revise it. It seems to me that whenever we become aware of how entirely controlled by it we believe ourselves to be, destined and fated and foreordained by it, there must come to us a certain sense of liberation when we remember our biological selves.

In fact, in viewing the animal Orwell may very well have found reason to assert the invulnerability of man. The possibility that worried him was not so much that humans might turn into animals but that the people who, like the proles, had maintained their instincts would become thoroughly civilized. Or to put it another way, one cannot afford to ignore, he argues, the unconscious morality of the clown-like dog that embarrasses the executioners in "A Hanging."

In *Animal Farm* Orwell illustrates—better than in any other work—both his affection for animals and his idea that certain civilizing influences threaten the moral dimension of the instincts; that "animals" may begin to resemble men until it is "impossible to say which [is] which." In light of this one can see that he makes use of the beast fable for two principal reasons: It provides a suitable vehicle for satire, and it is also thematically relevant. Animals are humorous in themselves, can serve as convenient metaphors for certain vices and virtues (pigs are greedy; donkeys, stubborn, and horses, hardworking, etc.), and finally, they can symbolize the positive, biological instincts. They are communal, loyal, and self-sacrificing. It is important to note in the satire that the animals' corruption results from contact with man or the tools of his civilization. Not until after they win the Battle of the Cowshed and fully assume Farmer Jones's place does injustice begin. The pigs, Snowball and Napoleon, weaken themselves by living in the farmhouse. And, importantly, the dogs, Bluebell, Jessie, and Pincher, are taken from their mother at birth and put through a form of brainwashing to turn them into brutal killers. Mollie, the foolish and vain mare, has been spoiled by Jones, and Moses, the conniving, clerical raven, has learned his theology from the outside world.

The point that Orwell makes here is not that the bare, natural instincts are politically or socially sufficient. He tended to believe, like the romantics, that man possessed inherent virtues which were the foundation for a moral life and which contemporary culture was bent on eliminating. This anarchistic aspect was, of course, present in his thought, but it should not be overemphasized. As I have continually stressed, he never asserted perfectibility inside, and certainly not outside, the social order; institutions, based on a conscious moral and historical sense, were required to give the person direction and order. Indeed, if in *Animal Farm* he symbolically suggests the ethical validity of the natural instincts, he also underlines how easily these instincts can be perverted. And if they are never totally obliterated—Benjamin, the donkey, survives on the periphery—they are, as in the proles, of little political value. In a situation like Animal Farm or Oceania, however, where almost every element of existence can be manipulated, if there is a hope it must lie in the uncontrollable, the nonrational. Here again Orwell's relationship with Lawrence as well as E.M. Forster is apparent. Although there are important differences in emphasis among them in this matter, all three felt that especially in a highly industrial and organized society the irrational and spontaneous elements in human character must be given play.

# *Animal Farm* Shows How Human Frailty Makes Successful Revolutions Unlikely

Roberta Kalechofsky

When Joseph Stalin, leader of the Soviet Union after the death of Vladimir Lenin, systematically eliminated people and groups that did not agree with his views and in effect turned the once-promising Russian "Socialist Paradise" into one more dictatorship, George Orwell and many other liberal supporters of the Russian Revolution were deeply disillusioned. How could this movement, which had promised to put all people on equal footing, have become twisted into the hellish totalitarian state it was by the late 1930s? *Animal Farm*, says Roberta Kalechofsky, is Orwell's response. Its characters—the greedy, power-hungry pigs and the passive or simple other animals—reflect society as Orwell saw it. A social revolution might be bound to fail, not because the ideology is wrong, but because people are flawed.

Orwell suggests that revolution is achieved in good measure through the power of slogans. His characters, divided into two basic types—the leaders (the pigs) and the followers (all the other animals)—create their revolution by following inspiring slogans such as "all animals are equal." But the greedy leaders gradually mutate the slogans and the simple followers do not notice as the changes are made. Soon, "some animals are more equal than others." The followers vaguely nod and continue following, while their equality erodes and the leaders become despots. Orwell's implication, says Kalechofsky, is that all revolutions may be doomed to failure. Orwell himself wrote in one of his essays, "In each great revolutionary struggle, the masses are led on by vague dreams of human brotherhood, and then, when the new ruling class is well established in power, they are thrust back into servitude."

Kalechofsky's books include *Autobiography of a Revolutionary: Essays on Animal and Human Rights* and *Jewish Writing from Down Under.*

Two questions dominate political thinking in this century. Why did a phenomenon like Hitler happen? Why did the Russian revolution fail? *Animal Farm* is concerned with the second question. From 1917 through the 1940s, Russia had been the lodestar for politically minded individuals who placed their hopes for social justice in radicalism and revolution. *Animal Farm* asks, allegorically, why the Russian revolution failed. The philosophical question behind the allegorical one is whether a morally successful revolution is ever possible.

*Animal Farm* will be Orwell's lasting achievement; it is the fable for twentieth-century political activists. The book is written so simply that it can be read in two hours by an adult and in four hours by a child. Like a Charlie Chaplin film, the inferences are complex and saturated with the history, the movements, and the thinking of this century; yet young and old, the sophisticated and the unsophisticated, can appreciate its plain and humanly appealing esthetic unity. *Animal Farm* has a pathos about the gullibility and insufficiency of human nature that speaks directly to its readers. . . .

The comedy—as well as the tragedy—in the book derives from the fact that the tale is about animals in revolt against man; therefore all the classical slogans of revolution take on wider significance. The cosmology broadens if one says, "down with man," rather than "off with the king's head," or "down with the tories." Major says that the answer to all their problems "is summed up in a single word—Man. Man is the only real enemy we have."

The main tenet of the revolutionary creed is that the animals are never to become like man. Major says to the animals, "And remember also that in fighting against Man, we must not come to resemble him. Even when you have conquered him, do not adopt his vices. . . . All the habits of Man are evil." The essential problem of revolution, as Orwell saw it, is how to combine power with ideals—how not to become like your oppressors were.

But failure of the social revolution is incipient in the nature of the animals and is apparent at this first meeting. Just as Major proclaims that "all animals are comrades," the dogs catch sight of four large rats and almost succeed in devouring them. Major calls for a vote on the issue. The majority agree that the rats too are comrades. There are four dissenting votes—the three dogs and the cat. Animal nature is already at work, destroying the possibility of social justice.

Major dies before the revolution. Napoleon, Snowball and Squealer busy themselves with elaborating Major's teachings into a system which they call Animalism. When the revolution does come, it comes unexpectedly and abruptly; it springs from the concrete experience of hunger, not from theories. Jones comes home drunk one night and forgets to feed the animals. He falls asleep with the *News of the World*

---

### *ANIMAL FARM*—PESSIMISM IN ACTION?

*Many have interpreted the conclusion of* Animal Farm *to suggest that all revolutions are doomed to failure. Here Orwell's colleague Laurence Brander comments on that idea in his 1954 book,* George Orwell.

The question one poses at the end of this fairy story is whether Orwell had given up hope that mankind would ever find decent government. It is very difficult here, as in *1984*, to decide. He had said in his essay on Swift that: "Of course, no honest person claims that happiness is *now* a normal condition among adult human beings; but perhaps it *could* be made normal, and it is upon this question that all serious political controversy really turns."

Essentially, *Animal Farm* is an anatomy of the development of the totalitarian State: "In each great revolutionary struggle the masses are led on by vague dreams of human brotherhood, and then, when the new ruling class is well established in power, they are thrust back into servitude."

It is a comment on all revolution: "History consists of a series of swindles, in which the masses are first lured into revolt by the promise of Utopia, and then, when they have done their job, enslaved over again by new masters."

Nothing is more obvious than where Orwell's sympathies lay. But whether he hoped that the common man could learn to find rulers is not clear. In *Animal Farm* he is an artist, posing great questions imaginatively; not a preacher, proclaiming a revelation.

over his face. Irresponsibility is his downfall. The starved animals panic and revolt. They attack the farm buildings and wipe out the reminders of Jones's tyranny—the nose rings, the dog chains, the halters, the blinkers, the nose bags, the whips. They change the name of Manor Farm to Animal Farm and set up seven commandments on the end wall of the big barn. Each of these commandments distinguishes animal nature from human nature.

1. Whatever goes upon two legs is an enemy.
2. Whatever goes upon four legs, or has wings, is a friend.
3. No animal shall wear clothes.
4. No animal shall sleep in a bed.
5. No animal shall drink alcohol.
6. No animal shall kill any other animal.
7. All animals are equal.

In time each maxim is corrupted. It is reworded to suit the needs of the pigs. Reality cannot be controlled by prophecies and proclamations. The corruptibility of language is indicated in the action of the cat who joins the Re-education Committee after the revolution and learns quickly that it is possible to use words for her own profit.

> She was seen one day sitting on a roof and talking to some sparrows who were just out of her reach. She was telling them that all animals were now comrades and that any sparrow who chose could come and perch on her paw; but the sparrows kept their distance.

## SEEDS OF DESTRUCTION

After the revolution most of the animals work very hard. Indeed, they work harder than they did under Jones's rule. Production is said to have improved, but the milk has been disappearing instead of being equally apportioned. Very early after the rebellion it is also discovered that the windfalls in the apple orchard are not being shared out. Squealer, the pig, pacifies the doubts of the animals: "'Comrades!' he cried. 'You do not imagine, I hope, that we pigs are doing this in a spirit of selfishness? . . . Our sole object in taking these things is to preserve our health.'" Gradually, the pigs move into Jones's house. It becomes known that they are eating in the kitchen and sleeping in beds. Remembering injunctions against such behavior, the animals rush to read the commandments. Number 4, contrary to memory, reads: "No animal shall sleep in a bed *with sheets.*"

Later, after celebrating a successful battle against the humans, Napoleon and the pigs get drunk. Again the animals rush to read the commandments, to check their memory. Now they discover that commandment number 5, contrary to what they thought, reads: "No animal shall drink alcohol *to excess.*" So it goes with each commandment.

The theme of the book is expressed not only by the corruption of the maxims, but by the fact that the degeneration of the revolution is measured by the progress the pigs make toward becoming more like man. The darkest aspect of the tragedy of social injustice is that the conquerors become what their oppressors were. Though Farmer Jones stages a counterrevolution that fails, the seeds for the destruction of the revolution are *within* the society itself. It is the "human nature" of the animals that defeats them.

# *Animal Farm* Shows the Evils of All Dictatorships

Alex Zwerdling

Karl Marx and Friedrich Engels published *The Communist Manifesto* in 1848. It described an ideal society in which all people would be equal, sharing both labor and resources. The proletarian, or working class, would be the norm—everyone would be a worker. There would be no kings or dictators, no inordinately rich people, and no poor. An inspiring document, its tenets were the basis of the Russian Revolution, the civil war in which the workers of Russia overthrew their oppressors and started a new, egalitarian society. Many outside Russia applauded the coup and viewed the new Russia as an Edenic state that would be a model for the world.

Within a very short time after the revolution in 1917, however, there began to be signs that the ideal would not be achieved. A trio of leaders—Joseph Stalin, Leon Trotsky, and Vladimir Lenin—were in charge, but when Lenin died in 1924, Stalin began a campaign to discredit and isolate Trotsky, whom he exiled in 1927. Stalin developed his power base and in the mid-1930s began a reign of terror in which he attempted to eliminate all "enemies of the state." During the purges of 1936–1938, Stalin's reign was responsible for the arrest of more than 7 million people and the execution of more than a half-million. This news could not be held inside the Soviet Union, and many of those who had viewed Russia idealistically, including Orwell, were disillusioned. While in service in Spain during the Civil War, his new views of Russian communism were reinforced: It had nothing to do with the socialist ideal he believed in.

Alex Zwerdling, an English professor who studied Orwell's relationship with and views of the Left (communism,

Marxism, socialism, and more) believes that Orwell's disillusionment with the Russian Revolution was only the starting point for *Animal Farm.* The book uses Russian history for its outline. But it is more than a criticism of Russia, says Zwerdling. It shows Orwell's disillusionment with other morally failed revolutions as well. It reflects Orwell's growing pessimism about the human condition as it relates to the outcome of idealistic revolutions.

In Orwell's speculations about revolution as a method for achieving socialist goals, he became far less confident than Trotsky that real progress was achieved through revolution, and his own view at times approaches Lord Acton's gloomy conviction that every revolution "makes a wise and just reform impossible." As early as 1938, the central idea of *Animal Farm* was running through Orwell's mind: "It would seem that what you get over and over again is a movement of the proletariat which is promptly canalised and betrayed by astute people at the top, and then the growth of a new governing class. The one thing that never arrives is equality. The mass of the people never get the chance to bring their innate decency into the control of affairs, so that one is almost driven to the cynical thought that men are only decent when they are powerless." Clearly Orwell still hesitates to accept this idea: he says he is "almost driven" to it. It remained an unresolved issue in his mind for years, and one can see why. His socialist faith made him need to deny it; his temperamental pessimism must have found it congenial. He could neither resolve the question nor forget it—perhaps the ideal condition for the creation of a vital literary work.

Orwell's uncertainty about revolution eventually produced *Animal Farm* and was responsible for the considerable ambiguity of the book. An ironic allegory is bound to mystify many of its readers, no matter how easy it is to identify the historical parallels on which it is based. We know that Orwell had a great deal of difficulty getting *Animal Farm* into print, and it is generally assumed that publishers rejected it because they did not want to publish an anti-Soviet satire in the middle of the war. Yet T.S. Eliot's letter of rejection from Faber makes it clear this was not the only problem the book raised. Eliot complains that "the effect is simply one of negation. It ought to excite some sympathy with what the author wants, as well as sympathy with his objections to something: and the positive point of view, which I take to be generally Trotskyite, is not convincing." He goes on to suggest that Orwell "splits his vote" by refusing to confirm any of the standard Western attitudes toward the Soviet Union.

## GENERAL ATTACK ON DICTATORSHIPS

Eliot's argument suggests a thoroughly confused sense of Orwell's purpose. If *Animal Farm* can be said to have a "positive point of view" at all, it is certainly not Trotskyite: Snowball is hardly its tragic hero. The difficulties of understanding *Animal Farm* largely stem from its interpretation as an exclusive attack on the Soviet Union. Orwell's purpose, however, is more general: he is interested in tracing the inevitable stages of any revolution, and he shapes his fable accordingly. This is not to deny that the literal level of the story is almost exclusively based on Soviet history. But although Russia is his immediate target, Orwell says the book "is intended as a satire on dictatorship in general." He was faithful to the details of Soviet history, yet he did not hesitate to transform some of its most important elements.

The most striking of these is the omission of Lenin from the drama. Major (the idealist visionary who dies before the revolution takes place) is clearly meant to represent Marx, while Napoleon and Snowball act out the conflict in the postrevolutionary state between Stalin and Trotsky. Lenin is left out, it seems to me, because Orwell wants to emphasize the enormous disparity between the ideals of the revolution and the reality of the society it actually achieves. Lenin was the missing link in this process, both visionary and architect of the new state, but from Orwell's longer historical perspective, his brief period of power must have seemed like an irrelevant interlude in the stark drama that was unfolding. The heirs of Lenin had in fact begun to transform him into a myth even before he was dead; they legitimized their power by worshipping at his shrine. In order to demythify the Russian Revolution and present the Bolshevik leaders as they really were, Orwell must have felt compelled to eliminate the mythical hero altogether.

Such radical departures from history are of course Orwell's prerogative in constructing a story intended to have more general significance. He says in a preface to *Animal*

*Farm* that "although the various episodes are taken from the actual history of the Russian Revolution, they are dealt with schematically and their chronological order is changed; this was necessary for the symmetry of the story." One might add that it was also necessary in order to achieve Orwell's purpose in writing it. This raises the question of how the topical and generic levels of satire in the book are related, and one might clarify the issue by citing the case of Jonathan Swift, who was in some sense Orwell's model.

## THE SAME VICES AND FOLLIES REIGN EVERYWHERE

When *Gulliver's Travels* was first published, many read the book as an essentially partisan political document, a propaganda piece for the opposition party. Yet Swift himself wrote to his French translator that, if *Gulliver's Travels* could only be understood in England, it was a failure, for "the same vices and the same follies reign everywhere . . . and the author who writes only for a city, a province, a kingdom, or even an age, deserves so little to be translated, that he does not even deserve to be read." In the same way, *Animal Farm* is concerned both with the Russian Revolution and, by extension, with the general pattern of revolution itself. As the Stalinist period recedes into the distant past, Orwell's book (if it survives as a literary work) will more and more be appreciated as generic rather than topical satire, just as *Gulliver's Travels* has come to be.

## STAGES OF REVOLUTION

Orwell chose to write his book in the form of a fable partly to give the pattern of historical events permanent mythic life, to emphasize that he was dealing with typical, not fortuitous, events. He is interested in constructing a paradigmatic social revolution, and the pattern that emerges is meant to apply to the Spanish Civil War and to the French Revolution (the main character, after all, is named Napoleon) as well as to the Russian one. Orwell's story suggests that revolutions inevitably go through several predictable stages. They begin with great idealistic fervor and popular support, energized by millennial expectations of justice and equality. The period immediately following a successful revolution is the Eden stage. There is a sense of triumphant achievement; idealistic vision is translated into immediate reality; the spirit of community and equality are everywhere apparent.

Old law and institutions are broken and replaced by an inner, yet reliable, concern for the common good. The state has, for the moment, withered away.

Slowly the feeling of freedom gives way to the sense of necessity and bondage, "we" becomes "I-they," spirit turns into law, improvised organization is replaced by rigid institutions, equality modulates to privilege. The next stage is the creation of a new elite which, because of its superior skill and its lust for power, assumes command and re-creates the class structure. Its power is first universally granted but gradually must be upheld against opposition by terror and threat. As time goes on, the past is forgotten or expunged; the new elite takes on all the characteristics of the old, prerevolutionary leadership, while the rest of the society returns to the condition of servitude. The transition is too gradual to be dramatic, although it has its dramatic moments, and it is constantly presented in the guise of historical inevitability or as a necessary response to conspiracy or external danger. A scapegoat is found to explain the disparity between ideal and actual. The exploited class remains exploited basically because of its doggedness and stupidity but also because, having no taste for power, it is inevitably victimized by the power-hungry. In every new society—even if it consists exclusively of those without previous experience of power—some will rise above their fellows and assume the available positions of authority. When their power and privileges are consolidated, they will fight to keep them. The only surviving vestiges of revolution will be its rhetoric and its (conveniently altered) history. The reality of "equality" and "justice" will have withered away, to be replaced by the state.

## HARD TRUTHS

"The effect," Eliot had said, "is simply one of negation." His objection raises the question of whether *Animal Farm* should be considered in moral terms at all. At this point in his career Orwell's mind had begun to work in an increasingly analytic way. He was interested in understanding the structure of revolution rather than in proposing a better way to achieve social goals. Eliot complains that the book fails to "excite some sympathy with what the author wants." Yet great satire has often been written out of the despairing sense that "what the author wants" may be unattainable. Orwell's socialism is not an act of faith. If he has a "positive point of view" at all in writing *Animal Farm*, it is the hope that socialists will be able to face the hard truths he presents rather than continue to accept the various consoling illusions their movement has generated to account for its disappointments.

And yet realism is not his only goal; he is also finally a moralist. In the essay on Dickens, Orwell makes an important distinction between the moralist and the revolutionary, which I take to be crucial for an understanding of his purpose in *Animal Farm*. Dickens, he says, is a moralist: "It is hopeless to try and pin him down to any definite remedy, still more to any political doctrine.... Useless to change institutions without a 'change of heart'—that, essentially, is what he is always saying." Orwell realized that the need for a "change of heart" has been used as "*the* alibi of people who do not wish to endanger the *status quo*," but he insists that this does not make Dickens a reactionary apologist. The paradox can only be explained by understanding the writer's relation to the moment in which he writes:

> I said earlier that Dickens is not *in the accepted sense* a revolutionary writer. But it is not at all certain that a merely moral criticism of society may not be just as "revolutionary"—and revolution, after all, means turning things upside down—as the politico-economic criticism which is fashionable at this moment. Blake was not a politician, but there is more understanding of the nature of capitalist society in a poem like "I wander through each charter'd street" than in three-quarters of Socialist literature. Progress is not an illusion, it happens, but it is slow and invariably disappointing. There is always a new tyrant waiting to take over from the old—generally not quite so bad, but still a tyrant. Consequently two viewpoints are always tenable. The one, how can you improve human nature until you have changed the system? The other, what is the use of changing the system before you have improved human nature? They appeal to different individuals, and they probably show a tendency to alternate in point of time.

## HISTORICAL PERSPECTIVE

The passage is remarkable for the sense it gives of Orwell's long historical perspective and his ability to see a particular artistic choice (Dickens's and, at this point, his own) as being in perpetual conflict with its equally legitimate opposite. The attitude could be described as dialectical, except that Orwell does not stress the synthesis which grows out of each clash. Rather, he sees the conflict as eternal: the point of view is far from the ultimate optimism of Hegel and Marx. At a particular moment in time, then, the moralist who voices his outrage at what is accepted, even though he has no idea how things might be changed, is more of a revolutionary than the "revolutionary" writer who endorses the most advanced form of social engineering. Most revolutionaries, as Orwell also points out in the Dickens essay, "are potential Tories, because they imagine that everything can be put right by altering the *shape* of society; once that change is effected, as it sometimes is, they see no need for any other."

It is at this moment—when a given revolution has more to preserve than to transform—that it is ripe for the moralist's exposé. Orwell felt that Soviet society had reached this stage, although most of the socialist camp still saw in it only its earlier, triumphant achievement. In performing this task, he hoped he might also make his audience aware that the illusion they cherished was only a particular example of a temptation they would meet again—the habit of substituting wish for reality.

It is, finally, impossible to talk about the political or moral purpose of *Animal Farm* without considering its tone. If the book is an exposé, it is certainly a remarkably unindignant one. Critics have praised its detachment, economy, and tight formal control; yet in a work with a serious political purpose, these qualities may not be as desirable as they are in purely aesthetic terms. There is truth in Mark Schorer's objection [in an early review of *Animal Farm*] that *Animal Farm* "undid its potential gravity and the very real gravity of its subject, through its comic devices." From the first page, Orwell's fable is marked by a sense of acceptance and composure. The satire is benevolent, the ridicule affectionate, the ingenuity and sophistication very far from impassioned preaching. It is as though the story of *The Revolution Betrayed* were retold a century later by a specialist in the ironies of history. Far more than *Nineteen Eighty-Four*, *Animal Farm* is written for posterity. The surprising thing is that it should have been the earlier book.

## INCONSISTENT TONE

To describe the tone of *Animal Farm* in a few phrases is to suggest that it is consistent. Yet there are important moments in the book when Orwell's comic perspective is quite clearly abandoned. For example: "Napoleon stood sternly surveying his audience; then he uttered a high-pitched whimper. Immediately the dogs bounded forward, seized four of the pigs by the ear and dragged them, squealing with pain and terror, to Napoleon's feet. The pigs' ears were bleeding, the dogs had tasted blood, and for a few moments they appeared to go quite mad." The passage stands at the beginning of the scene meant to parallel the Stalinist purge trials, and it is typical of the tone of gravity Orwell employs to describe the reign of terror that now begins at Animal Farm. The purge trials are the first events in Soviet history that Orwell considers tragically. Although terror was not, of course, invented by Stalin, there is something about the Moscow Trials which Orwell cannot treat as a predictable part of his paradigmatic revolution, something new in human history. It is, perhaps, the triumph of the big lie in Napoleon's justification for this slaughter of the innocents, the false confessions and abandonment of objective truth it involves. Here was something Orwell could not treat with composure and ironic detachment.

Orwell's tone in both *Animal Farm* and *Nineteen Eighty-Four* is determined by his sense of the uniqueness or typicality of the events he records. As long as he describes what he considers an inevitable stage of revolution, he can allow himself the long, detached historical perspective and the ironic tone that is its aesthetic correlative. When, on the other hand, he senses that some new, unexpected, and therefore perhaps avoidable form of tyranny has appeared, his response is very different: he permits himself the indignation of first discovery. . . .

In order to understand Orwell's growing pessimism in the 1940s, it is worth recalling the fundamentally optimistic elements that still formed a part of his commitment to socialism at the beginning of the decade. His very guarded faith in the future rested on three assumptions: first, that although every revolution is betrayed and falls far short of its original goals, in the long view "progress is not an illusion"; second, that every oppressive regime is eventually destroyed by the people it oppresses; and third, that human greed and lust for power are probably not permanent impulses of human nature but are historically determined by the condition of scarcity and the competitive ethic it spawns.

## THE TERROR OF MODERN DICTATORSHIPS

The events of the late thirties and forties seemed to provide evidence that not even these vaguely hopeful beliefs could survive objective scrutiny. What observer of the methods of totalitarian rule in Russia and Germany could continue to believe in the slow but inevitable march of progress? As Orwell put it in his essay on H.G. Wells, "Creatures out of the Dark Ages have come marching into the present." Only those who had lived under a totalitarian regime seemed able to grasp the extraordinary atavism of modern tyranny. The Russian writer Yevgeny Zamyatin, whose novel of the future, *We*, greatly influenced Orwell in the conception of *Nineteen Eighty-Four*, had taken account of "the diabolism & the tendency to return to an earlier form of civilisation which seem to be part of totalitarianism." Zamyatin's book, Orwell says, gives the regime of the future "the colour of the sinister slave civilisations of the ancient world" and shows an "intuitive grasp of the irrational side of totalitarianism—human sacrifice, cruelty as an end in itself, the worship of a Leader who is credited with divine attributes."

More frightening even than this reversal of progress was the idea that such regimes might prove invulnerable to revolution. Orwell first mentions this possibility in 1939, in a review of a book about the Soviet Union that preached the inevitability of a new Russian revolution. In disputing this theory, Orwell is also calling into question the optimistic conclusion of *The Revolution Betrayed:*

> The terrifying thing about the modern dictatorships is that they are something entirely unprecedented. Their end cannot be foreseen. In the past every tyranny was sooner or later overthrown, or at least resisted, because of "human nature", which as a matter of course desired liberty. But we cannot be at all certain that "human nature" is constant. It may be just as possible to produce a breed of men who do not wish for liberty as to produce a breed of hornless cows.

The growth of a movement resisting an oppressive state depends on certain conditions that a totalitarian regime might well succeed in stamping out. Its control of every aspect of human life narrowed the areas of independence its subjects could enjoy. Modern communication systems vastly increased the possibility of surveillance and thought-control. Previous autocratic societies had been full of interstices the state did not enter, small pockets of privacy in which a man or a small group of men could work out rebellious ideas and plans in some safety. Furthermore, the modern centralized apparatus of dictatorship—its control of the press, of publishing houses, of the schools, and all other organizations—gave it an unprecedented opportunity to indoctrinate its subjects. . . .

It was entirely possible, then, that the totalitarian regimes of the twentieth century would be permanent rather than subject to the historical process. Marx had said that after the socialist revolution, history could begin. It seemed to Orwell more likely that after a revolution leading to the creation of a totalitarian state, history might end. The invention of atomic weapons made this more likely, since they served to make powerful states invulnerable to external attack. Hitler was finally overthrown only by losing a world war. Might the Nazi state still exist if German scientists had perfected the atomic bomb before or at the same time as their enemies? Although the three superstates in *Nineteen Eighty-Four* wage a limited kind of war incessantly, it is "warfare of limited aims between combatants who are unable to destroy one another, have no material cause for fighting and are not divided by any genuine ideological difference." What hope is there for oppressed people in such countries?

Furthermore, one of the most "progressive" aspects of totalitarian regimes made their tyranny potentially more stable than the "reactionary" systems they had replaced—the fact that power and privilege were not hereditary. Hereditary institutions, Orwell suggests, "have the virtue of being unstable. They must be so, because power is constantly devolving on people who are either incapable of holding it, or use it for purposes not intended by their forefathers. It is impossible to imagine any hereditary body lasting so long, and with so little change, as an adoptive organisation like the Catholic Church. And it is at least thinkable that another adoptive and authoritarian organisation, the Russian Communist Party, will have a similar history."

Such a state is less likely to become decadent than its predecessors, first because it can secure the most able recruits from all sectors of society, thus simultaneously making it an aristocracy of talent and depriving the powerless of potential leaders, and second because it can eliminate from its ranks all decadent, untrustworthy, or incompetent members. . . .

The adoptive rather than hereditary autocracy of totalitarianism created another, even more serious threat to human happiness: it encouraged and rewarded the power-mad. As Bertrand Russell had argued in *Power,* "Where no social institution, such as aristocracy or hereditary monarchy, exists to limit the number of men to whom power is possible, those who most desire power are, broadly speaking, those most likely to acquire it. It follows that, in a social system in which power is open to all, the posts which confer power will, as a rule, be occupied by men who differ from the average in being exceptionally power-loving." Of course this might equally be said of a democracy in which elective office is open to all, but at least in such governments there are some safeguards against the worst abuses of power, safeguards a totalitarian state does not have. This fear that the world would be taken over by the power-mad became the most serious and persistent obsession of Orwell's last years. As long as the existence of privilege could be explained along economic lines, as a necessary condition when there was not enough to go around, the future offered some hope for a solution. But to Orwell it began to seem more and more likely that money was merely a distraction on the road to power, and that the desire for power was an appetite which could of necessity never be satisfied universally.

The displacement of greed by sadistic power-hunger seemed to Orwell a modern phenomenon that could only flourish once a certain level of universal comfort was attainable. Perhaps it could be understood as a postcapitalist phase: "Just as at the end of the feudal age there appeared a new figure, the man of money, so at the end of the capitalist age there appears another new figure, the man of power, the Nazi gauleiter or Bolshevik commissar. Such men may be individually corrupt, but as a type they are neither mercenary nor hedonistic. They don't want ease and luxury, they merely want the pleasure of tyrannising over other people." If this theory was true, the socialist might well despair of his faith. He was taught to interpret oppression as an economic rather than a psychological fact. Yet at the very moment in human history when economic oppression is no longer a necessity for the survival of the few, equality seems more unattainable than ever. The demand for absolute power over others, Orwell writes in 1946, "has reached new levels of lunacy in our own age." This leads him to a question he could never answer: "What is the special quality in modern life that makes a major human motive out of the impulse to bully others?"

The apparently irresistible cult of power brought Orwell to a deeper despair than any of his previous observations.

Although he cannot explain its etiology, he records its triumphs in essay after essay written in the 1940s, and finally, of course, in *Nineteen Eighty-Four*. Orwell was particularly shaken by the realization that the worship of power was not merely limited to those anxious to exercise it. The totalitarian state satisfied many of the led as well as the leaders because the relationship seemed to fulfill a deep psychological need. The "cult of personality" spoke to some primitive instinct both in Germany and in the Soviet Union, despite the rebellious disaffection of the few. The true modern myth, Orwell says in "Raffles and Miss Blandish," "should be renamed Jack the Dwarf-killer." The two-minute hate sessions in *Nineteen Eighty-Four*, the love for and identification with Big Brother, even Winston's fantasies while being tortured, are all based on this insight. Winston and O'Brien forge a symbiotic bond. As he awakes after a scene of terrible torture, Winston is amazed to find that he feels no hatred: "The pain was already half-forgotten. He opened his eyes and looked up gratefully at O'Brien. At sight of the heavy, lined face, so ugly and so intelligent, his heart seemed to turn over. If he could have moved he would have stretched out a hand and laid it on O'Brien's arm. He had never loved him so deeply as at this moment."

What hope was there for the ideals of socialism, "equality" and "the classless society," when such powerful psychological forces were released and then systematically exploited? Orwell's growing despair clearly arose from thwarted optimism. His socialist faith began with a need to find a system that would provide an end to "every form of man's dominion over man." But if the victim is also in some crucial sense an accomplice, the whole theory of the need to support the oppressed against the oppressor takes on the character of an elaborate delusion: it is like interfering in a lovers' quarrel.

# *Animal Farm* Is a Strong Political Allegory

Jeffrey Meyers

Orwell "felt it was his vocation to warn men about the future," writes Jeffrey Meyers in the introduction to the book from which this viewpoint is excerpted. In *Animal Farm*, Meyers asserts, Orwell warns of the deception and failure of the Communist Revolution in Russia, a revolution that had been a beacon of hope in the eyes of most liberals of the first half of the twentieth century. Communism had promised equality to all people and sharing of resources and the profits resulting from their use. But with the Stalinist purges of the 1930s, it became clear that the revolution had failed. True, the Russian people were no longer subjects of the czar, but the leaders who had replaced the royal family had turned out to have their own selfish and exploitative agenda. People were not free unless they believed and did exactly as the Party wanted; resources were not shared in an egalitarian way. Stalin and others proved that Communist leaders were just as power hungry as any dictator.

Orwell felt bound to expose the evils of communism because at the time he wrote the book Communist Russia was an ally of the Western powers. People seemed blind to what was happening there and to the Soviet Union's potential for expansion at the cost of free peoples in the countries around it. To wake people up, Orwell wrote *Animal Farm*, which, Meyers points out, has an incredible number of parallels to the events that had occurred in the USSR during the previous decades. Not only can parallels be discovered by the reader by referring to recent history, but Orwell himself spoke to his purpose. Meyers points out several of Orwell's comments regarding this.

Excerpted from Jeffrey Meyers, *A Reader's Guide to George Orwell* (London: Thames & Hudson, 1975). Reprinted with permission of Thames & Hudson and of Rowman & Littlefield.

Jeffrey Meyers is the author of more than thirty-five biographies and books on literature, three of them on George Orwell.

Orwell believes that "The business of making people *conscious* of what is happening outside their own small circle is one of the major problems of our time, and a new literary technique will have to be evolved to meet it." His choice of a satiric beast fable for *Animal Farm* (1945) was exactly what he needed, for his creation of characters was always rather weak, and the flat symbolic animals of the fable did not have to be portrayed in depth. The familiar and affectionate tone of the story and its careful attention to detail allowed the unpopular theme to be pleasantly convincing, and the Soviet myth was exposed in a subtle fashion that could still be readily understood. It was written in clear and simple language that could be easily translated, and was short so that it could be sold cheaply and read quickly. The gay *genre* was a final attempt to deflect his profound pessimism, which dominated his final realistic vision of decency trampled on and destroyed in *1984*.

Experimentation with the literary techniques that could most forcefully convey his ideas is characteristic of all Orwell's non-fiction: autobiographical, sociological, and political. Though he had considerable success as a polemicist and pamphleteer, this *genre* was too blunt and too direct, for his views were extremely unpopular at the time he expressed them. *Animal Farm* was written between November 1943 and February 1944, after Stalingrad and before Normandy, when the Allies first became victorious and there was a strong feeling of solidarity with the Russians, who even in retreat had deflected Hitler from England. Distinguished writers like Wells, Shaw, Barbusse and Rolland had praised Russia highly. But Orwell's book belongs with Trotsky's *The Revolution Betrayed* (1937), Gide's *Return from the U.S.S.R.* (1937) and Koestler's *Darkness at Noon* (1941), three prescient attacks on the Stalinist régime; and it anticipates postwar denunciations like Crossman's compilation *The God That Failed* (1949) and Djilas' *The New Class* (1957).

Orwell had defined the theme of his book as early as "Inside the Whale" (1940); and he writes in his essay on James Burnham (1946), "History consists of a series of swindles, in which the masses are first lured into revolt by the promise of Utopia, and then, when they have done their job, enslaved over again by new masters." In his Preface to the Ukrainian edition of *Animal Farm* (1947), he states that

> The man-hunts in Spain went on at the same time as the great purges in the USSR and were a sort of supplement to them.... Nothing has contributed so much to the corruption of the original idea of Socialism as the belief that Russia is a Socialist country and that every act of its rulers must be excused, if not imitated. And so for the past ten years I have been convinced that the destruction of the Soviet myth was essential if we wanted a revival of the Socialist movement.

## EVERY DETAIL SIGNIFICANT

... Though critics have often interpreted the book in terms of Soviet history, they have never sufficiently recognized that it is extremely subtle and sophisticated, and brilliantly presents a satiric allegory of Communist Russia in which virtually every detail has political significance.

Orwell describes the creative impulse of the book in his Preface:

> I saw a little boy, perhaps ten years old, driving a huge cart-horse along a narrow path, whipping it whenever it tried to turn. It struck me that if only such animals became aware of their strength we should have no power over them, and that men exploit animals in much the same way as the rich exploit the proletariat. I proceeded to analyse Marx's theory from the animals' point of view.

Major's speech is an accurate exposition of orthodox Marxism and is very similar to the last paragraph of the *Communist Manifesto* (1848): the Communists

> openly declare that their ends can be attained only by the forcible overthrow of all existing social conditions. Let the ruling classes tremble at the Communistic revolution. The proletarians have nothing to lose but their chains. They have a world to win. WORKINGMEN OF ALL COUNTRIES, UNITE!

In his *Critique of the Gotha Program*, Marx stated, "From each according to his abilities, to each according to his needs"; and when Animal Farm is established, "everyone worked according to his capacity." And Squealer's ingenious gloss on "Four legs good, two legs bad" is a witty and ironic example of specious Marxist polemics: "A bird's wing, comrades ... is an organ of propulsion and not of manipulation. It should therefore be regarded as a leg."

"Comrade Napoleon," the poem of Minimus (who is based

on the Russian poet Mayakovsky) is a close imitation of adulatory Soviet verse like the [anonymous] "Hymn to J.V. Stalin":

> The world has no person
> Dearer, closer,
> With him, happiness is happier,
> And the sun brighter. . . .

And parts of the revolutionary song, "Beasts of England," closely paraphrase certain lines of [the Communist anthem] "L'Internationale" (1871). "L'Internationale" expresses the brief but idealistic exhilaration that Orwell experienced under the short-lived Anarchist government in Barcelona. As he wrote to Cyril Connolly from Spain in 1937, "I have seen wonderful things & at last really believe in Socialism, which I never did before."

Immediately after the pigs celebrate their victory and bury "some hams hanging in the kitchen" (a wonderful detail), the revolutionary principles of Major are codified by Snowball into "The Seven Commandments." The corruption inherent in the Rebellion is manifested as each of the Commandments is successively betrayed, until none of the original revolutionary idealism remains. As in Orwell's early novels and *1984*, the structure of the books is circular, and by the time the name is changed back to Manor Farm, there has been a return to the *status quo* (or worse) with whisky and whips in the trotters of the pigs.

## ORWELL SIMILARITIES

In the Preface to *Animal Farm*, Orwell writes: "Although various episodes are taken from the actual history of the Russian Revolution, they are dealt with schematically and their chronological order is changed." Thus, the human beings are capitalists, the animals are Communists, the wild creatures who could not be tamed and "continued to behave very much as before" are the *muzhiks* or peasants, the pigs are the Bolsheviks, the Rebellion is the October Revolution, the neighbouring farmers are the western armies who attempted to support the Czarists against the Reds, the wave of rebelliousness that ran through the countryside afterwards is the abortive revolutions in Hungary and Germany in 1919 and 1923, the hoof and horn is the hammer and sickle, the Spontaneous Demonstration is the May Day celebration, the Order of the Green Banner is the Order of Lenin, the special pig committee presided over by Napoleon is the Politbureau, the revolt of the hens—the *first* rebellion since the expulsion of Jones (the Czar)—is the sailors' rebellion at the Kronstadt naval base in 1921, and Napoleon's dealings with Whymper and the Willingdon markets represent the Treaty of Rapallo, signed with Germany in 1922, which ended the capitalists' boycott of Soviet Russia.

### PARALLELS WITH RUSSIAN HISTORY

*Clearly,* Animal Farm *has drawn strongly from Russian twentieth-century history. In the table below, literary scholar John Atkins provides an easy reference list of some of the most obvious parallels.*

Critical discussion of *Animal Farm* has tended to concentrate largely on its satirical and allegorical elements. Certainly there are close parallels between the plot of the book and the history of the USSR between 1917 and 1943, and the book should be examined carefully for such parallels. The numerous symbolisms may be expressed in tabular form, as follows:

| | |
|---|---|
| Mr Jones | Tsar Nicholas II |
| Major | Marx |
| Boxer | The Proletariat |
| Napoleon | Stalin |
| Snowball | Trotsky |
| Squealer | *Pravda* |
| Minimus | Mayakovsky |
| The Pigs | The Bolsheviks |
| Moses | The Russian Orthodox Church |
| Mollie | The White Russians |
| Pilkington | Britain |
| Frederick | Germany |
| The farmhouse | The Kremlin |
| The Rebellion | The Russian Revolution |
| The Battle of the Cowshed | The allied invasion of 1918–19 |
| The Battle of the Windmill | The German invasion of 1941 |
| The windmill | The Five-Year Plans |
| "Beasts of England" | "L'Internationale" |

The carefully chosen names are both realistic and highly suggestive of their owners' personalities and roles in the fable. The imperious Major (Marx-Lenin) is military, dominant and senior (in public school jargon); the rather stupid and self-sacrificing Boxer (the proletariat), who is contrasted to the cynical Benjamin and the indifferent and unenthusiastic cat, is named after the Chinese revolutionaries who drove out foreign exploiters and were themselves crushed; Mollie (the White Russians) suggests folly, and her retrogressive defection for vanity and luxury is a paradigm of the entire revolution; Moses (the Russian Orthodox and later the Catholic Church) brings divine law to man; Squealer (a living *Pravda*) is onomatopoetic for a voluble pig; and Whymper, the pigs' agent, suggests a toady. Pilkington (Churchill-England), the capitalist exploiter, connotes "bilk" and "milk" (slang): he is an old-fashioned gentleman who enjoys country sports on Foxwood, which has associations of both craftiness and the Tory landed gentry. Frederick (Hitler) refers to Frederick the Great, the founder of the Prussian military state and Hitler's hero. Frederick is a tough, shrewd man who drives hard bargains, steals other people's land for his own farm, Pinchfield, and practices terrible cruelties upon his subjects. These cruelties are related to the most moving scene in the novel—when Boxer is taken to the slaughter-house—for the knacker's van recalls the terrible gas vans used by the *Einsatzgruppen* for mobile extermination. Though Clover screams out, "They are taking you to your death," the sound of Boxer's drumming hoofs inside the van "grew fainter and died away."

## REVOLUTIONS BECOME DICTATORSHIPS

The most important animals are Napoleon (Stalin) and Snowball (Trotsky), whose personalities are antithetical and who are never in agreement. Both characters are drawn fully and accurately, though with simple strokes, and reflect almost all the dominant characteristics of their historical models. Like Trotsky, Orwell compares Stalin to Napoleon, for both turned revolutions into dictatorships (Bonapartism was the successor to Thermidor), both transformed a national popular "revolution from below" into a foreign conqueror's "revolution from above," and both forcibly imposed their revolutionary ideology on other countries. Napoleon the pig is fierce-looking, "not much of a talker, but with a reputation for getting his own way." He dominates the party machinery, controls the education of the young and is superb at plotting and "canvassing support for himself" between meetings. Napoleon never presents any of his own plans and always criticizes Snowball's, though he eventually adopts these plans and even claims he invented them. He first distorts and then changes history, blames Snowball for all his own failures, accuses him of plotting with foreign enemies, drives him into exile and finally pronounces his death sentence. He also publishes fantastic production figures, takes "credit for every successful achievement and every stroke of good fortune," wins elections unanimously, names cities after himself and replaces the cult of Major ("the animals were required to file past the skull [Lenin's Tomb] in a reverent manner") with a more elaborate one of his own. As Orwell writes in 1941, "One could not have a better example of the moral and emotional shallowness of our time, than the fact that we are now all more or less pro-Stalin. This disgusting murderer is temporarily on our side, and so the purges etc. are suddenly forgotten."

The name Snowball recalls Trotsky's white hair and beard, and the fact that he melted before Stalin's opposition. Snowball is a brilliant speaker, sometimes unintelligible to the masses but always eloquent and impressive, more vivacious and inventive than Napoleon, and a much greater writer. He is also intellectual and energetic. For, as Deutscher writes of Trotsky in 1921, besides running the army and serving on the Politbureau,

> He was busy with a host of other assignments each of which would have made a full-time job for any man of less vitality and ability. He led, for instance, the Society of the Godless. . . . He was at this time Russia's chief intellectual inspirer and leading literary critic. He frequently addressed audiences.

Orwell's description of Snowball's activities, though a comic parody, is close to reality:

> Snowball also busied himself with organising the other animals into what he called Animal Committees. . . . He formed the Egg Production Committee for the hens, the Clean Tails League for the cows, the Wild Comrades Re-education Committee . . . and various others, besides instituting classes in reading and writing.

Snowball studies military history, organizes, commands and leads the Army to victory in the Battle of the Cowshed (the Civil War) where foreign powers help Mr Jones and invade the farm (Russia). After the War he was "full of plans for innovation and improvements."

Two of the most important battles between Trotsky and Stalin are allegorized in the novel. Trotsky fought for the priority of manufacturing over agriculture and for accelerated

industrialization, and his ideas for the expansion of the Socialist sector of the economy were eventually adopted by
Stalin in the first five-year plan of 1928, which called for collectivization of farms *and* for industrialization: "Snowball
conjured up pictures of fantastic machines which would do
their work for them while they grazed at their ease in the
fields . . . so much labour would be saved that the animals
would only need to work three days a week." Stalin wanted
comprehensive and drastic collectivization: Napoleon "argued that the great need of the moment was to increase food
production, and that if they wasted time on the windmill
they would all starve to death."

## PERMANENT REVOLUTION

In their central ideological conflict, Trotsky defended his
idea of "Permanent Revolution" against Stalin's theory of
"Socialism in One Country." Historian Isaac Deutscher
writes that "Two rival and quasi-Messianic beliefs seemed
pitted against one another: Trotskyism with its faith in the
revolutionary vocation of the proletariat of the West; and
Stalinism with its glorification of Russia's socialist destiny."
Orwell presents this controversy in simpler but entirely accurate words:

> According to Napoleon, what the animals must do was to pro-
> cure firearms and train themselves in the use of them. Ac-
> cording to Snowball, they must send out more and more pi-
> geons and stir up rebellion among the animals on the other
> farms. The one argued that if they could not defend them-
> selves they were bound to be conquered, the other argued
> that if rebellions happened everywhere they would have no
> need to defend themselves.

When Snowball comes to the crucial points in his speeches,
"It was noticed that [the sheep] were especially liable to
break into 'Four legs good, two legs bad,'" just as in the party
Congress in 1927, at Stalin's instigation, "pleas for the opposition were drowned in the continual, hysterically intolerant
uproar from the floor [Deutscher]." The Trotsky-Stalin conflict reached a crucial point in mid-1927, after Britain broke
diplomatic relations with Russia and ruined Stalin's hopes
for an agreement between Soviet and British trade unions;
the Russian ambassador to Poland was assassinated; and
Chiang Kai-shek massacred the Chinese Communists who
had joined him at Stalin's orders. Trotsky and the Opposition
issued a declaration attacking Stalin for these political and

military failures, but before they could bring this issue before the party Congress and remove Stalin from power, he expelled Trotsky and Zinoviev from the Party. Orwell writes of this vital moment in Soviet history, which signalled the final defeat of Trotsky, "By the time he [Snowball] had finished speaking, there was no doubt as to the way the vote would go. But just at this moment" Napoleon's dogs (the GPU, or Secret Police) attacked Snowball and forced him to flee the farm and go into exile.

Orwell is not primarily interested in the practical or ideological merits of these controversies, for he believed (wrongly, I think) that *both* men had betrayed the revolution. He told a friend that "Trotsky-Snowball was potentially as big a villain as Stalin-Napoleon, although he was Napoleon's victim. The first note of corruption was struck when the pigs secretly had the cows' milk added to their own mash and Snowball consented to this first act of inequity." And he writes in 1939, the year before Trotsky's murder, "It is probably a good thing for Lenin's reputation that he died so early. Trotsky, in exile, denounces the Russian dictatorship, but he is probably as much responsible for it as any man now living, and there is no certainty that as a dictator he would be preferable to Stalin, though undoubtedly he has a much more interesting mind."

## Strangest Parallels

The three main Russian political events that are most extensively allegorized in *Animal Farm* are the disastrous results of Stalin's forced collectivization (1929–33), the Great Purge Trials (1936–38) and the diplomacy with Germany that terminated with Hitler's invasion in 1941. Orwell writes that "after Snowball's expulsion, the animals were somewhat surprised to hear Napoleon announce that the windmill was to be built after all." The first demolition of the windmill, which Napoleon blames on Snowball, is the failure of the first five-year plan. The destructive methods of the hens during the "Kronstadt Rebellion"—they "made a determined effort to thwart Napoleon's wishes. Their method was to fly up to the rafters and there lay their eggs, which smashed to pieces on the floor"—are precisely those used by the *muzhiks* in 1929 to protest against the forced collectivization of their farms: "In desperation they slaughtered their cattle, smashed implements, and burned crops. This was the *muzhiks'* great Luddite-like rebellion [Deutscher]." The result of this enormous ruin was, as Orwell writes in a 1938 review of Lyons's book on Russia, "years of appalling hardship, culminating in the Ukraine famine of 1933, in which a number estimated at not less than three million people starved to death." Deutscher mentions the recurrent cannibalism during times of starvation, and Orwell refers to this famine when he writes, "It was being put about that all the animals were dying of famine and disease . . . and had resorted to cannibalism and infanticide."

## THE PURGES

The most dramatic and emotional political events of the thirties were the Great Purge Trials, the minute details of which were published in the official translation of 1938. Stalin's motive, according to the editors of the trials' transcript, was a craving "to achieve an unrestricted personal dictatorship with a totality of power that he did not yet possess in 1934." They also state that in the trial "pieces of falsified real history have been woven along with outright fiction." A perfect example of this occurs when the animals "remembered that at the critical moment of the battle Snowball had turned to flee," but forgot that it was a deliberate ruse to prepare the victorious ambush.

In the trial of Trotsky's friend Karl Radek, in February 1937, the prosecution claimed that Trotsky

> was organizing and directing sabotage in the Soviet Union, catastrophes in coal mines, factories, and on the railways, mass poisonings of Soviet workers, and repeated attempts on the lives of Stalin and other members of the Politbureau.

After the destruction of the windmill, Napoleon roars:

> thinking to set back our plans . . . this traitor has crept here under cover of night and destroyed our work of nearly a year. . . .

> A rumour went round that Snowball had after all contrived to introduce poison into Napoleon's food.

In the last and most important trial, that of Bukharin in March 1938, Gorky's secretary Kryuchkov confessed, "I arranged long walks for Alexie Maximovich, I was always arranging bonfires. The smoke of the bonfire naturally affected Gorky's weak lungs." During the purge in *Animal Farm*, "Two other sheep confessed to having murdered an old ram, an especially devoted follower of Napoleon, by chasing him round and round a bonfire when he was suffering from a cough."

In his review of Lyons's book, Orwell is horrified by the "monstrous state trials at which people who have been in prison for months or years are suddenly dragged forth to make incredible confessions"; and, in his satire, "A sheep confessed to having urinated in the drinking pool—urged to do this, so she said, by Snowball." Historians Herbert Tucker and Stephen Cohen state that nine million people were arrested during the purges, and that the number of people executed has been reliably estimated at three million. In *Animal Farm*, all the "guilty" animals are "slain on the spot," and in a terrifying moment of the book, after the confessions and executions, "there was a pile of corpses lying before Napoleon's feet and the air was heavy with the smell of blood."

## DECEPTIVE DIPLOMACIES

After solidifying his domestic power through massive liquidation, Stalin turned his attention to the increasing menace in Europe and attempted to play off the democracies against Hitler. Deutscher describes how

> He still kept his front doors open for the British and the French and confined the contact with the Germans to the back stairs.... It is still impossible to say confidently to which part of the game Stalin then attached the greatest importance: to the plot acted on the stage or to the subtle counter-plot.

Similarly, the animals were amazed when they discovered that, during Napoleon's apparent friendship with Pilkington, he "had really been in secret agreement with Frederick." But Napoleon is sadly deceived: Frederick's bank notes (the Hitler-Stalin non-aggression pact of August 1939) are forgeries, and he attacks Animal Farm without warning and destroys the windmill. Orwell's letter to his publisher in 1945 gives a fascinating insight into the precision of his allegorical technique:

> When the windmill is blown up, I wrote "all the animals including Napoleon flung themselves on their faces." I would like to alter it to "all the animals except Napoleon." If the book has been printed it's not worth bothering about, but I just thought the alteration would be fair to Joseph Stalin, as he did stay in Moscow during the German advance.

Hitler's defeat in the Battle of Stalingrad (January 1943) was the turning point of the Russian campaign: when the enemy "saw that they were in danger of being surrounded, Frederick shouted to his men to get out while the going was good, and the next moment the cowardly enemy was running for dear life."

One of Stalin's diplomatic blunders is also portrayed by Orwell. The reappearance of the raven Moses "after an absence of several years" and his eternal talk about the Sugarcandy Mountain represents Stalin's queer attempt, in the spring of 1944, at reconciliation with the Pope. In order to gain Catholic support for his Polish policy, he received a lowly and unaccredited American priest, Father Orlemanski, and "was twice closeted with him for long hours" during a most crucial period of the war. Nothing came of this, of course, and the result of this stunt, writes Deutscher, was that Stalin was made "the laughing-stock of the world."

The satire concludes, as Orwell says in the Preface, with the 1943 "Teheran Conference, which was taking place while I was writing." Deutscher, who knew him, relates that Orwell was "unshakably convinced that Stalin, Churchill, and Roosevelt consciously plotted to divide the world, and to divide it for good, among themselves, and to subjugate it in common. . . . '*They* are all power-hungry,' he used to repeat." The disagreement between the allies and the beginning of the cold war is symbolized when Napoleon and Pilkington, both suspicious, "played an ace of spades simultaneously."

## PERVASIVE, BRILLIANT ALLEGORY

The political allegory of *Animal Farm*, whether specific or general, detailed or allusive, is pervasive, thorough and accurate, and the brilliance of the book becomes much clearer when the satiric allegory is compared to the political actuality. Critics who write, "it makes a delightful children's story" and who emphasize that "the gaiety in his nature had completely taken charge" are dimly unaware of the allegory's sophisticated art. Orwell wrote to Middleton Murry the year he finished the work, "I consider that willingness to criticise Russia and Stalin is *the* test of intellectual honesty," and by his own or any standard it is an honest and even a courageous book.

Though subtle and compressed, *Animal Farm* shares the serious theme of *Nostromo*: that once in power, the revolutionary becomes as tyrannical as his oppressor. For Orwell writes of the post-revolutionary farm:

In the old days there had often been scenes of bloodshed

equally terrible, but it seemed to all of them that it was far worse now that it was happening among themselves.

And Dr. Monygham similarly condemns the cruel and unprincipled capitalistic revolutionaries:

> They have their law, and their justice. But it is founded on expediency, and is inhuman; it is without rectitude, without the continuity and the force that can be found only in a moral principle. The time approaches when all that . . . [it] stands for shall weigh as heavily upon the people as the barbarism, cruelty, and misrule of a few years back.

# *Animal Farm* Exposes Orwell's Sexism

Daphne Patai

In her preface to the book from which this viewpoint is excerpted, Daphne Patai writes of her longtime interest in Orwell. When she was beginning her research, she says, a colleague asked her what attracted her to Orwell. She responded that she was drawn to Orwell's passion and honesty. Upon much reflection and research, however, she reassessed her view. "I came to see that a passion for appearing honest and actually being honest are very different things," she wrote, "and that saying what one thinks can be as much an act of aggression as a display of lofty principles." In *Animal Farm*, Patai argues, Orwell depicts the oppression of one socioeconomic class by another, but he gives only a partially honest picture: He shows the class of pigs (like the class of politically powerful humans) oppressing the class of all the other animals (comparable to all the people who are not politically powerful). Yet he completely ignores a more pervasive kind of oppression—that of females by males. Thus, he has only limited honesty, and his oblivious passion helps perpetuate the oppression of more than half the human race. She concludes, "In the future, I think, interest in Orwell will focus not on his work but on the phenomenon of his fame and what it reveals about our civilization"— like Orwell, our civilization blindly ignores the plight of oppressed females.

Patai teaches Spanish and Portuguese at the University of Massachusetts, Amherst. She has written several books on Brazilian literature, as well as *Professing Feminism: Cautionary Tales from the Strange World of Women's Studies.*

Reprinted from *The Orwell Mystique: A Study of Male Ideology*, by Daphne Patai (Amherst: University of Massachusetts Press, 1984), copyright ©1984 by Daphne Patai, by permission of the publisher.

116

Although *Animal Farm* is mentioned in scores of studies of Orwell, no critic has thought it worth a comment that the pigs who betray the revolution, like the pig who starts it, are not just pigs but boars, that is, uncastrated male pigs kept for breeding purposes. Old Major, the "prize Middle White boar" who has called a meeting to tell the other animals about his dream, is initially described in terms that establish him as patriarch of this world: "He was twelve years old and had lately grown rather stout, but he was still a majestic-looking pig, with a wise and benevolent appearance in spite of the fact that his tushes had never been cut." In contrasting his life with those of the less fortunate animals on the farm, Major says: "I am one of the lucky ones. I am twelve years old and have had over four hundred children. Such is the natural life of a pig." Orwell here repeats the pattern we have seen in his other fiction, of stressing paternity as if the actual labor of reproduction were done by males. Authority comes from the phallus and fatherhood, and the sows, in fact, are hardly mentioned in the book; when they are, as we shall see, it is solely to illustrate the patriarchal control of the ruling pig, Napoleon. Leaders, then, may be good (Major) or bad (Napoleon)—but they must be male and "potent."

Contrasting with the paternal principle embodied in Major is the maternal, embodied in Clover, "a stout motherly mare approaching middle life, who had never quite got her figure back after her fourth foal." Clover is characterized above all by her nurturing concern for the other animals. When a brood of ducklings that had lost their mother come into the barn, Clover "made a sort of wall round them with her great foreleg," and they nestled down inside it. Though Clover works along with Boxer—the enormous cart horse "as strong as any two ordinary horses put together" whom Orwell uses to represent the working class, unintelligent but ever-faithful, to judge by this image—she is admired not for her hard labor but rather for her caring role as protector of the weaker animals. Orwell here attributes to the maternal female dominion over the moral sphere but without any power to implement her values. As in *Nineteen Eighty-Four,* this "feminine" characteristic, though admirable, is shown to be utterly helpless and of no avail. In addition, this conventional (human) division of reality restricts the female animal to the affective and expressive sphere and the male to the instrumental.

## AMBIVALENT IMAGERY

Orwell at times utilizes the same imagery in opposing ways; imagery relating to passivity, for example, is presented as attractive in "Inside the Whale" and repulsive when associated with pansy pacifists. This ambivalence is demonstrated as well in Orwell's use of protective maternal imagery. Clover's protective gesture toward the ducklings, viewed positively in *Animal Farm,* is matched by Orwell's ridicule of a similar image in his verse polemic with Alex Comfort in 1943, about half a year before Orwell began composing *Animal Farm.* Falling into his familiar tough-guy rhetoric, Orwell angrily defended Churchill against pacifist gibes. . . . The protective environment must be rejected if manly status is to be preserved. But the protective gesture itself, in its inevitable futility, is admired in *Animal Farm,* and it is through Clover that Orwell expresses the sadness of the failed revolution after the "purges" occur, as the stunned animals huddle around her:

> As Clover looked down the hillside her eyes filled with tears. If she could have spoken her thoughts, it would have been to say that this was not what they had aimed at when they had set themselves years ago to work for the overthrow of the human race. These scenes of terror and slaughter were not what they had looked forward to on that night when old Major first stirred them to rebellion. If she herself had had any picture of the future, it had been of a society of animals set free from hunger and the whip, all equal, each working according to his capacity, the strong protecting the weak, as she had protected the last brood of ducklings with her foreleg on the night of Major's speech.

Clover is here contrasted with Boxer, who is unable to reflect on these matters and simply resolves to work even harder than before. Though Clover too "would remain faithful, work hard, carry out the orders that were given to her, and accept the leadership of Napoleon," she has the moral awareness to know that "it was not for this that she and all the other animals had hoped and toiled." But she lacks the words to express this awareness and instead sings "Beasts of England."

Clover stands at one of the poles of Orwell's conventional representation of female character. The other pole is represented by Mollie, "the foolish, pretty white mare who drew Mr Jones's trap" and is shown, early in the book, to have a link with human females. When the animals wander through the farmhouse, Mollie lingers in the best bedroom: "She had taken a piece of blue ribbon from Mrs Jones's dressing-table, and was holding it against her shoulder and admiring herself in the glass in a very foolish manner." A less important female character is the cat who, during Major's speech, finds the warmest place to settle down in and does not listen to a word he says. Both Mollie and the cat, we later learn, avoid work; and Mollie is the first defector from the farm after the revolution, seduced by a neighboring farmer's offerings of ribbons for her white mane and sugar.

Orwell's characterizations of old Major, Boxer, Clover, Mollie, and the cat all appear, clearly packaged and labeled, in the book's first three pages. The animal community thus forms a recognizable social world, divided by gender. This world is presented to us complete with stereotypes of patriarchal power, in the form of male wisdom, virility, or sheer strength, and female subordination, in the form of a conventional dichotomy between "good" maternal females and "bad" nonmaternal females. It is difficult to gauge Orwell's intentions in making use of gender stereotypes in *Animal Farm*. Given the evidence of his other texts, however, it seems unlikely that the possibility of a critical, even satirical, account of gender divisions ever crossed his mind. Perhaps he simply incorporated the familiar into his animal fable as part of the "natural human" traits needed to gain plausibility for his drama of a revolution betrayed. But in so doing he inadvertently reveals something very important about this barnyard revolution: Like its human counterparts, it invariably re-creates the institution of patriarchy.

## SEXUAL POLITICS ON THE FARM

Not only does Orwell's satire of a Marxist ("Animalist") revolution fail to question gender domination while arguing against species domination, it actually depends upon the stability of patriarchy as an institution. This is demonstrated by the continuity between Mr. Jones, the original proprietor of the farm, and Napoleon (Stalin), the young boar who contrives to drive out Snowball (Trotsky), the only competing boar on the premises, and assumes Jones's former position as well as that of Major, the old patriarch.

In her study of feminism and socialism [*The Curious Courtship of Women's Liberation and Socialism*], Batya Weinbaum attempts to explain why socialist revolutions have tended to reestablish patriarchy. Describing this pattern in the Russian and Chinese revolutions, Weinbaum utilizes the terminology of kin categories: father, daughter, brother, wife. These categories allow her to point out that revolutions have expressed the revolt of brothers against fathers. Though her analysis relies on a Freudian model of sexual rivalry, agreement about motivation is not necessary in order to see the value of the kin categories she proposes. While daughters participate along with brothers in the early stages of revolution, they are increasingly left out of the centers of power once the brothers realize they can occupy the positions formerly held by the fathers, thus gaining privileged access to the labor and services of women.

It is intriguing to note how closely this scheme fits *Animal Farm*. Although Orwell describes a generalized revolt of the animals, inspired by a wise father's message of freedom, this revolt against the human exploiter Jones is quickly perverted into a struggle between two of the brothers, each eager to occupy the father slot and eliminate his competitor. Orwell makes it explicit that the struggle goes on between the only two boars among the pigs. The male porkers (castrated pigs) are not contenders for the father role. There is even an especially nasty portrayal of Squealer, the public relations porker who, in keeping with Orwell's other slurs against the press, is depicted as devoid of masculinity (in Orwell's terms): He stays safely away from the fighting. Once Napoleon wins out over Snowball, we see just what the father role means in terms of access to females. As the sole potent male pig on the farm, Napoleon is of course the father of the next generation of elite pigs: "In the autumn the four sows had all littered about simultaneously, producing thirty-one young pigs between them. The young pigs were piebald, and as Napoleon was the only boar on the farm, it was possible to guess at their parentage."

In addition, the relations among the sows, competing for Napoleon's favor, are hinted at near the story's end, when Napoleon is on the verge of complete reconciliation with the human fathers, the neighboring farmers. Orwell informs us that the pigs (males) began to wear Mr. Jones's clothes, "Napoleon himself appearing in a black coat, ratcatcher breeches, and leather leggings, while his favourite sow appeared in the watered silk dress which Mrs. Jones had been used to wearing on Sundays." Perhaps because these details seem to be beside the point in terms of the allegory, they are all the more intriguing as instances of Orwell's fantasy at work. Intentionally or not, Orwell has re-created the structure of the patriarchal family. As in human families, power among the pigs is organized along two axes: sex and age.

## MALES SHOWN AS SUPERIOR

Though we are told that the pigs as a whole exploit the other animals (by keeping more and better food for themselves, claiming exemption from physical labor because they are doing the "brainwork" of the farm, and finally moving into the farmhouse and adopting all the formerly proscribed human habits), it is only the male pigs whom we see, in the book's closing line, as indistinguishable from human males: "The creatures outside looked from pig to man, and from man to pig, and from pig to man again; but already it was impossible to say which was which." Piggish adaptation to the human world involves not only the general class discrimination evident in the rewritten Commandment: "All animals are equal but some animals are more equal than others." It also appears more specifically in the gender hierarchy that culminates in this last scene, so different from the account of the revolution itself in which virtually all the animals and both sexes had participated.

Even as the animal allegory duplicates Orwell's gender assumptions, it also liberates him to some extent from the confines of his own androcentric framework. This is apparent in the unfolding of old Major's speech early in the book. He begins with general comments about the animals' lot: "No animal in England knows the meaning of happiness or leisure after he is a year old. No animal in England is free. The life of an animal is misery and slavery: that is the plain truth." But as he continues to speak, his emphasis shifts slightly:

> Why then do we continue in this miserable condition? Because nearly the whole of our produce is stolen from us by human beings. There, comrades, is the answer to all our problems. It is summed up in a single word—Man. Man is the only real enemy we have. Remove Man from the scene, and the root cause of hunger and overwork is abolished forever.

> Man is the only creature that consumes without producing. He does not give milk, he does not lay eggs, he is too weak to pull the plough, he cannot run fast enough to catch rabbits.

Here, for the first and only time in his writings, Orwell rec-

ognizes female reproductive labor as part and parcel of a society's productive activities and as a form of labor that gives
females the right to make political and economic demands.
In old Major's speech, it is this female labor, specifically,
that becomes the most dramatic focal point. The passage
quoted above continues:

> Yet he [Man] is lord of all the animals. He sets them to work,
> he gives back to them the bare minimum that will prevent
> them from starving, and the rest he keeps for himself. Our
> labour tills the soil, our dung fertilizes it, and yet there is not
> one of us that owns more than his bare skin. You cows that I
> see before me, how many thousands of gallons of milk have
> you given during this last year? And what has happened to
> that milk which should have been breeding up sturdy calves?
> Every drop of it has gone down the throats of our enemies.
> And you hens, how many eggs have you laid this year, and
> how many of those eggs ever hatched into chickens? The rest
> have all gone to market to bring in money for Jones and his
> men. And you, Clover, where are those four foals you bore,
> who should have been the support and pleasure of your old
> age? Each was sold at a year old—you will never see one of
> them again. In return for your four confinements and all your
> labour in the field, what have you ever had except your bare
> rations and a stall?

In this passage Orwell is finally able to make the connection
between "public" and "private"—between the male's (typical) work of production and the female's (typical) work of
reproduction. He sees that both forms of labor can be expropriated and that the "private" sphere in which relations of
caring and nurturing go on is very much a part of the over-
all system of exploitation that old Major protests. Thinking
about animals, Orwell notices that females are insufficiently
rewarded for the labor stolen from them by men.

### EXPLOITING FEMALES

As the revolution decays, there occurs an episode in which
Napoleon forces the hens to give up more of their eggs, so
that they can be used for export to a neighboring farm. At
first the hens sabotage this plan by dropping their eggs from
the rafters of the barn. But they are quickly brought into line
by the cessation of their rations (the acquisition of food still
not being under their direct control). After holding out for
five days, the hens capitulate. This increased expropriation
of the hens' products is viewed by Orwell in precisely the
same terms as the increased labor time extracted from the

other animals. In contrast, when Orwell wrote about the human working class, he never noticed the economics of reproduction or objected to women's exclusion from direct access to decent livelihoods—an exclusion justified by reference to their status as females and supposed dependents of males. It is as if, since his farm animals are not divided into individual family groupings, Orwell was able to break through the ideology of "typical family" that had earlier blinded him to the reality of women's work and position in capitalist society.

In *Animal Farm,* furthermore, Orwell touches on the problem of political expropriation of female reproductive capacity. Napoleon provides himself with a secret police force by separating a litter of newborn puppies from their mothers and rearing them himself, and these puppies, when grown up, drive out the rival brother, Snowball, and inaugurate Napoleon's reign of terror. Orwell here seems to protest against the breakup of the "natural" pattern by which the pups are suckled and raised by their mothers. This theme is reiterated when Napoleon seizes the thirty-one young pigs—his offspring—and appoints himself their instructor, so as to prepare the continued domination of pigs over the other animals in the future. Such "unnatural" expropriations stand in sharp opposition to the traditional patterns of family life so strongly supported by Orwell. The same sort of "state" interference in family life occurs, in more detailed form, in *Nineteen Eighty-Four.*

Although his fiction suggests a strong distaste for these examples of state expropriation of female reproductive labor, Orwell was actually urging the adoption in England of population policies that, if put into practice, would have openly treated women as mere vehicles for fulfilling state priorities. In "The English People," written in 1944 (that is, shortly after *Animal Farm)* though not published until 1947, Orwell, in the throes of a panic about the dwindling birthrate, exhorts the English to have more children as one of the necessary steps in order to "retain their vitality." Interpreting the declining birthrate primarily as an economic problem, he urges the government to take appropriate measures:

> Any government, by a few strokes of the pen, could make childlessness as unbearable an economic burden as a big family is now: but no government has chosen to do so, because of the ignorant idea that a bigger population means

more unemployed. Far more drastically than anyone has proposed hitherto, taxation will have to be graded so as to encourage child bearing and to save women with young children from being obliged to work outside the home.

In addition to economic and social incentives, Orwell says, a "change of outlook" is needed: "In the England of the last thirty years it has seemed all too natural that blocks of flats should refuse tenants with children, that parks and squares should be railed off to keep the children out of them, that abortion, theoretically illegal, should be looked on as a peccadillo, and that the main aim of commercial advertising should be to popularise the idea of 'having a good time' and staying young as long as possible."

## "BREED FASTER, WORK HARDER"

In brief, what the English must do is, among other things, to "breed faster, work harder, and probably live more simply," a program ominously reminiscent of Napoleon's exhortation to the other animals: "The truest happiness, he said, lay in working hard and living frugally." In Orwell's concern with socially adequate human breeding there is no more consideration for the choices of women than Napoleon shows for the desires of the hens or bitches whose eggs and puppies he removes. Orwell seems to assume that the "natural" desires of women will precisely coincide with the lines he sets out— if, that is, he has paused to look at the matter from their point of view at all. Several years later, Orwell still viewed the "population problem" in the same terms. In a newspaper column in 1947, he voices alarm that, if England does not quickly reach an average family size of four children (instead of the then existing average of two), "there will not be enough women of child-bearing age to restore the situation." He worries about where future workers will come from and again recommends financial incentives. Though Orwell was hardly alone in expressing such concerns at that time, it is instructive to note the limited perspective he brings to the problem. And yet in *Nineteen Eighty-Four* he satirizes the Party's control over Outer Party members' reproductive behavior through the character of Winston's wife, Katharine, who chills Winston's blood with her commitment to regular sexual intercourse as an expression of "our duty to the Party." It seems obvious that Orwell's opinion of such state interference in sex and procreation has nothing to do with any sympathy for women as individuals but depends entirely upon his judgment of the merits of the state that is being served.

Nothing in Orwell's earlier writings reveals an awareness of the economic contributions made by women as reproducers, rearers, and caretakers of the labor force, not to mention as ordinary members of the work force. It is therefore all the more surprising that in letting his imagination translate human conflicts into animal terms this aspect of female roles at once sprang to his attention. At the same time, his female animals are still rudimentary in comparison with the more subtly drawn portraits of the male animals on the farm. The hens and cows, for example, appear primarily as good followers, prefiguring Orwell's description of Outer Party female supporters in *Nineteen Eighty-Four*. With the exception of the maternal Clover and, to a lesser extent, Mollie, the female animals are unimportant as individual actors in the fable. . . .

As the pigs duplicate the human model of social organization, they not only reproduce the pattern of patriarchy already familiar to the animals (judging by Major's status early in the book) but add to it those human characteristics that Orwell found most reprehensible—especially softness. They slowly adopt Mr. Jones's manner of living, complete with cushy bed and booze. This is contrasted with the heroic labor of the immensely strong Boxer, who literally works himself to death. Relations between the pigs and the other animals follow the patriarchal model also in that they are hierarchical and discipline-oriented; submission and obedience are extracted from the worker animals as the price of the supposedly indispensable pig leadership.

## MALE BONDING

In addition to the touching solidarity evident among the worker animals, some individual relationships also emerge. One of these is the nonverbal "masculine" friendship between Boxer and Benjamin, who look forward to their retirement together. There is no female version of this friendship, however. Instead, Clover plays the role not only of maternal mare to the other animals but also of "wife"—to use Weinbaum's kin categories again—in that she has a heart-to-heart talk with Mollie. Cast in the role of the rebellious "daughter" who refuses to adhere to the farm's values, Mollie disbelieves in the communal cause and prefers to ally herself with powerful human males outside the farm, thus assuring her easier life as a kept and well-decorated mare. Orwell signals his disapproval of Mollie by showing her cowardice as well as her vanity and sloth. Given the revolution's eventual outcome, however, Mollie's behavior, though egocentric, is not as misguided as it may seem. Orwell makes it explicit that under the rule of Napoleon the animals (except the pigs and Moses, the raven, who represents the church) have an even more arduous work life than animals on the neighboring (i.e., capitalist) farms. Mollie might better be viewed as having some spontaneous understanding of the rules of patriarchy, characterized by Weinbaum in these words: "Brothers may step across the line to become fathers; but daughters face a future as a powerless wife.". . .

It is fascinating to see Orwell describe the betrayal of the animals' revolution in terms so suggestive of women's experience under patriarchy. It is women who, more than any other group and regardless of the race and class to which they belong, have had their history obliterated, their words suppressed and forgotten, their position in society confounded by the doublethink of "All men are created equal," their legal rights denied, their labor in the home and outside of it expropriated and controlled by men, their reproductive capacities used against them, their desire for knowledge thwarted, their strivings turned into dependence—all of these under the single pretext that they are not "by nature" equipped to do the valued work of society, defined as what men do. When read as a feminist fable, however, *Animal Farm* has another important message. The origins of the Seven Commandments of Animalism lie in Major's warnings against adopting Man's ways: "And remember also that in fighting against Man, we must not come to resemble him. Even when you have conquered him, do not adopt his vices."

# Orwell Was "the Wintry Conscience of a Generation"

V.S. Pritchett

By the time of George Orwell's death in 1950, he had achieved a significant amount of fame. He had been writing literary and political essays for years, and he had published two international best-sellers in his last five years—*Animal Farm* and *1984*. He had developed many friends and admirers along the way. One of the most powerful tributes to him was written by Sir Victor Pritchett, a fellow book reviewer. While Pritchett may go too far in describing Orwell as a kind of saint, he does delineate many of the qualities that have made Orwell and his works live on long beyond his death.

George Orwell was the wintry conscience of a generation which in the 'thirties had heard the call to the rasher assumptions of political faith. He was a kind of saint and, in that character, more likely in politics to chasten his own side than the enemy. His instinctive choice of spiritual and physical discomfort, his habit of going his own way, looked like the crankishness which has often cropped up in the British character; if this were so, it was vagrant rather than puritan. He prided himself on seeing through the rackets, and on conveying the impression of living without the solace or even the need of a single illusion.

There can hardly have been a more belligerent and yet more pessimistic Socialist; indeed his Socialism became anarchism. In corrupt and ever worsening years, he always woke up one miserable hour earlier than anyone else and, suspecting something fishy in the site, broke camp and advanced alone to some tougher position in a bleaker place; and it had often happened that he had been the first to de-

From V.S. Pritchett, Obituary, *New Statesman & Nation*, January 28, 1950. Reprinted by permission of Guardian News Service Ltd., London.

tect an unpleasant truth or to refuse a tempting hypocrisy. Conscience took the Anglo-Indian out of the Burma police, conscience sent the old Etonian among the down and outs in London and Paris, and the degraded victims of the Means Test or slum incompetence in Wigan; it drove him into the Spanish civil war and, inevitably, into one of its unpopular sects, and there Don Quixote saw the poker face of Communism. His was the guilty conscience of the educated and privileged man, one of that regular supply of brilliant recalcitrants which Eton has given us since the days of Fielding; and this conscience could be allayed only by taking upon itself the pain, the misery, the dinginess and the pathetic but hard vulgarities of a stale and hopeless period.

But all this makes only the severe half of George Orwell's character. There were two George Orwells even in name. I see a tall emaciated man with a face scored by the marks of physical suffering. There is the ironic grin of pain at the ends of kind lips, and an expression in the fine eyes that had something of the exalted and obstructive farsightedness one sees in the blind; an expression that will suddenly become gentle, lazily kind and gleaming with workmanlike humour. He would be jogged into remembering mad, comical and often tender things which his indignation had written off; rather like some military man taking time off from a private struggle with the War Office or society in general.

He was an expert in living on the bare necessities and a keen hand at making them barer. There was a sardonic suggestion that he could do this but you could not. He was a handyman. He liked the idea of a bench. I remember once being advised by him to go in for goat-keeping, partly I think because it was a sure road to trouble and semistarvation; but as he set out the alluring disadvantages, it seemed to dawn on him that he was arguing for some country Arcadia, some Animal Farm, he had once known; goats began to look like escapism and, turning aside as we walked to buy some shag at a struggling Wellsian small trader's shop, he switched the subject sharply to the dangerous Fascist tendencies of the St John's Wood Home Guard who were marching to imaginary battle under the Old School Tie.

As an Old School Tie himself, Orwell had varied one of its traditions and had 'gone native' in his own country. It is often said that he knew nothing about the working classes, and indeed a certain self-righteousness in the respectable working class obviously repelled his independent mind. So many of his contemporaries had 'gone native' in France; he redressed a balance. But he did know that sour, truculent, worrying, vulgar lower class England of people half 'done down,' commercially exploited, culturally degraded, lazy, feckless, mild and kind who had appeared in the novels of Dickens, were to show their heads again in Wells and now stood in danger of having the long Victorian decency knocked out of them by gangster politics.

## THE HOPE OF 'THE PEOPLE'

By 'the people' he did not mean what the politicians mean; but he saw, at least in his Socialist pamphlets, that it was they who would give English life of the future a raw, muddy but unmistakable and inescapable flavour. His masochism, indeed, extended to culture.

In a way, he deplored this. A classical education had given him a taste for the politician who can quote from Horace; and as was shown in the lovely passages of boyhood reminiscence in *Coming Up for Air,* his imagination was full only in the kind world he had known before 1914. Growing up turned him not exactly into a misanthrope—he was too good-natured and spirited for that—but into one who felt too painfully the ugly pressure of society upon private virtue and happiness. His own literary tastes were fixed—with a discernible trailing of the coat—in that boyish period: Bret Harte, Jules Verne, pioneering stuff, Kipling and boys' books. He wrote the best English appreciation of Dickens of our time. *Animal Farm* has become a favourite book for children. His Burmese novels, though poor in character, turn Kipling upside down. As a reporting pamphleteer, his fast, clear, grey prose carries its hard and sweeping satire perfectly.

He has gone; but in one sense, he always made this impression of the passing traveller who meets one on the station, points out that one is waiting for the wrong train and vanishes. His popularity, after *Animal Farm,* must have disturbed such a lone hand. In *1984,* alas, one can see that deadly pain, which had long been his subject, had seized him completely and obliged him to project a nightmare, as Wells had done in his last days, upon the future.

# Chronology

**1903**

June 25—Eric Arthur Blair is born in Motihari, Bengal, India, to Richard Walmesley Blair, a subdeputy opium agent in the Indian Civil Service, and Ida Mabel Blair (nee Limouzin); the Blairs have one other child, Marjorie Frances, who was born 1898; December 17—Wright brothers' first flight

**1904**

Ida, Eric, and Marjorie move to Henley on Thames, England; Richard remains in India

**1905**

The start of the Russian Revolution

**1906**

First Labour Party forms in England; earthquake devastates parts of San Francisco

**1907**

Rudyard Kipling wins Nobel prize for literature

**1908**

Eric's sister Avril Nora is born

**1911**

Eric attends St. Cyprian's, a private boarding school in Eastbourne, Sussex

**1912**

Richard Blair retires from opium department; family resettles in Shiplake, near Henley on Thames; *Titanic* sinks

**1914**

Eric's poem "Awake, Young Men of England" is published in local newspaper; assassination of archduke Francis Ferdinand of Austria causes outbreak of World War I

**1915**

Blairs move back to Henley on Thames; Albert Einstein's *General Theory of Relativity* is published

**1916**

In December Eric leaves St. Cyprian's

**1917**

In May Eric enters Eton as King's Scholar; Russian czar is overthrown and Bolsheviks come to power during the October Revolution; Vladimir Ilyich Lenin becomes chief commissar

**1918**

Armistice ends World War I

**1919**

Benito Mussolini founds fascist movement in Italy. Mohandas Gandhi begins program of peaceful resistance against British government in India; Prohibition begins in United States

**1920**

League of Nations is established

**1921**

Eric leaves Eton; family moves to Southwold, a seaside resort in Suffolk; British Broadcasting Corporation (BBC) is founded

**1922**

In October Eric joins Indian Imperial Police in Mandalay, Burma; Egypt wins independence from Great Britain; Union of Soviet Socialist Republics (U.S.S.R.) is established

**1923**

William Butler Yeats wins Nobel prize for literature; Adolf Hitler is imprisoned for his failed attempt to overthrow Bavarian government

**1924**

Lenin dies; Joseph Stalin takes control of U.S.S.R.; First Labour government established in England

**1925**

Hitler's autobiography, *Mein Kampf,* is published

## 1927

After leaving Imperial Police, Eric returns to England in August and goes "tramping" in London's East End; Charles Lindbergh makes first solo flight around the world

## 1928

Eric goes to Paris; in October his first professional article is published in *Le Monde;* in December his first published article in England appears in *G.K.'s Weekly*

## 1929

Eric develops pneumonia and spends several weeks in hospital; returns to England in the fall; Wall Street crash leads to worldwide economic depression

## 1930

Eric begins writing regularly for the literary journal *Adelphi;* in October Eric finishes draft of *Down and Out in Paris and London,* which is rejected by several publishers before Victor Gollancz accepts it; Eric works as private schoolmaster and tutor

## 1931

Eric begins writing *Burmese Days*

## 1932

Eric begins teaching in private school in Hayes, West London

## 1933

Gollancz publishes *Down and Out in Paris and London,* Eric assumes pseudonym George Orwell, although he never legally changes his name; Orwell develops pneumonia in December and leaves teaching position; Hitler becomes chancellor of Germany; Spanish government puts down anarchist uprisings; Prohibition ends in United States

## 1934

Orwell begins writing *A Clergyman's Daughter* while convalescing at parents' home in Southwold; In October *Burmese Days* is published in New York; Orwell takes part-time job in bookshop in London; Stalinist purge of Communist Party and Russian army begins in U.S.S.R.

## 1935

Orwell begins work on *Keep the Aspidistra Flying;* meets Eileen O'Shaughnessy

**1936**

Orwell researches lifestyle of poor in Wigan, Liverpool, Manchester, and Barnsley; Orwell and Eileen marry on June 9; English king George V dies; Edward VII abdicates throne "to be with the woman he loves"; Italy annexes Ethiopia; after start of Spanish Civil War, Orwell enlists in militia of the Workers' Party of Marxist Unification in Spain; Francisco Franco becomes head of fascist government

**1937**

Orwell is shot in throat while serving in Spain in May; returns to England and writes *Homage to Catalonia*, but Gollancz refuses to publish it, fearing it will harm fight against fascism; Fredric Warburg agrees to publish work; Orwell turns against Stalinist Communism but continues to support socialist ideals

**1938**

Orwell develops tubercular lesion in lung and enters sanatorium in Kent; spends winter in Morocco with Eileen; Hitler annexes Austria; takes one-third of Czechoslovakia; Volkswagen, ballpoint pens, and instant coffee come into being

**1939**

In June Orwell's father, Richard Blair, dies of cancer at age 82; World War II breaks out; Orwell is rejected as medically unfit; Eileen works in Censorship Department; Madrid falls to Franco; Spanish Civil War ends; Germany and U.S.S.R. sign nonaggression pact; Germany attacks Poland; England and France declare war on Germany; U.S.S.R. attacks Poland

**1940**

Orwell joins Home Guard; begins writing *The Lion and the Unicorn*, which calls for an English revolution; contributes to *Horizon* magazine; Winston Churchill becomes prime minister of Great Britain; Russian Communist leader Leon Trotsky is assassinated in Mexico; Franklin D. Roosevelt is elected to third term as U.S. president

**1941**

In August Orwell joins BBC as a producer for programs to India; writes "London Letters" for *Partisan Review;* Japanese attack Pearl Harbor; United States joins war; Orson Welles's film *Citizen Kane* debuts

## 1942

Orwell continues to work at the BBC; writes for many publications, including *Horizon, Partisan Review, New Statesman and Nation,* and the *Observer;* Battle of Stalingrad begins between Germans and Russians; first controlled, self-sustaining nuclear reaction takes place at the University of Chicago; first surface-to-surface guided missile test at Peenemünde, Germany, by engineer Wernher von Braun

## 1943

In March Orwell's mother, Ida Blair, dies of heart attack; In November Orwell resigns from BBC, starts writing *Animal Farm;* joins socialist journal *Tribune* as literary editor; begins weekly column "As I Please" for *Tribune;* Germans surrender at Stalingrad

## 1944

Orwell finishes *Animal Farm;* starts frustrating hunt for publishers, who shy from it for political reasons; Warburg finally agrees to publish the work; Eileen quits her job and the Orwells adopt a three-week-old boy they name Richard Horatio Blair; D-Day; liberation of Paris; Roosevelt elected to fourth term

## 1945

Orwell quits his job at *Tribune;* travels to France to write for *Observer;* Eileen dies under anesthesia during a hysterectomy; *Animal Farm* is published; Orwell travels to the Hebridean island of Jura, where he takes an extended vacation; Roosevelt dies; Harry S. Truman becomes president of the United States; Hitler commits suicide; Mussolini is assassinated; war in Europe ends; United States bombs Hiroshima, Japan, and ends the war in the Pacific; United Nations is formed

## 1946

Orwell's sister Marjorie, 48, dies of kidney disease in May; Orwell moves to a farmhouse on Jura; Avril comes to stay; *Animal Farm* is published in New York and bought by the Book-of-the-Month Club, which sells half a million copies; Orwell begins working on *1984*

## 1947

Orwell is diagnosed with tuberculosis in December; India is given independence from Britain

**1948**

Orwell finishes final draft of *1984* in December while seriously ill; Gandhi is assassinated; independent state of Israel is founded; first Arab-Israeli war begins

**1949**

In June *1984* is published; Book-of-the-Month buys it also; In September Orwell is admitted to University College Hospital; In October, he marries Sonia Brownell, an editorial assistant at *Horizon*, in special hospital ceremony; Communists take over China

**1950**

January 21—Orwell dies of pulmonary tuberculosis at age 46; buried in All Saints churchyard in the village of Sutton Courtenay, Oxfordshire, England

# FOR FURTHER RESEARCH

Keith Alldritt, *The Making of George Orwell*. London: Edward Arnold, 1969.

Laurence Brander, *George Orwell*. New York: Longmans, Green, 1954.

Jacintha Buddicom, *Eric and Us: A Remembrance of George Orwell*. London: Leslie Frewin of London, 1974.

Jenni Calder, *Chronicles of Conscience: A Study of George Orwell and Arthur Koestler*. London: Secker and Warburg, 1968.

Audrey Coppard and Bernard Crick, *Orwell Remembered*. New York: Facts On File, 1984.

Bernard Crick, *George Orwell: A Life*. London: Secker and Warburg, 1980.

T.R. Fyvel, *George Orwell: A Personal Memoir*. London: Weidenfeld and Nicolson, 1982.

Averil Gardner, *George Orwell*. Boston: Twayne, 1987.

Miriam Gross, ed., *The World of George Orwell*. London: Weidenfeld and Nicolson, 1971.

J.R. Hammond, *A George Orwell Companion*. New York: St. Martin's, 1982.

Christopher Hollis, *A Study of George Orwell: The Man and His Work*. London: Hollis and Carter, 1956.

Tom Hopkinson, *George Orwell*. London: Longmans, Green, 1965.

Lynette Hunter, *George Orwell: The Search for a Voice*. Milton Keynes, England: Open University Press, 1984.

Stephen Ingle, *George Orwell: A Political Life*. New York: Manchester University Press, 1993.

Roberta Kalechofsky, *George Orwell*. New York: Frederick Ungar, 1973.

David L. Kubal, *Outside the Whale: George Orwell's Art and Politics*. Notre Dame: University of Notre Dame Press, 1972.

Robert A. Lee, *Orwell's Fiction*. Notre Dame: University of Notre Dame Press, 1969.

Jeffrey Meyers, *George Orwell: The Critical Heritage*. Boston: Routledge & Kegan Paul, 1975.

———, *A Reader's Guide to George Orwell*. London: Thames and Hudson, 1975.

Valerie Meyers, *Modern Novelists: George Orwell*. New York: St. Martin's, 1991.

Robert Mulvihill, ed., *Reflections on America, 1984: An Orwell Symposium*. Athens: University of Georgia Press, 1986.

Christopher Norris, ed., *Inside the Myth: Orwell: Views from the Left*. London: Lawrence and Wishart, 1984.

Bernard Oldsey and Joseph Browne, *Critical Essays on George Orwell*. Boston: G.K. Hall, 1986.

Daphne Patai, *The Orwell Mystique: A Study in Male Ideology*. Amherst: University of Massachusetts Press, 1984.

Patrick Reilly, *George Orwell: The Age's Adversary*. New York: St. Martin's, 1986.

John Rodden, *The Politics of Literary Reputation: The Making and Claiming of 'St. George' Orwell*. New York: Oxford University Press, 1989.

Michael Shelden, *Orwell: The Authorized Biography*. New York: HarperPerennial, 1992.

Christopher Small, *The Road to Miniluv: George Orwell, the State, and God*. London: Victor Gollancz, 1975.

Richard I. Smyer, *Animal Farm: Pastoralism and Politics*. Boston: Twayne, 1988.

———, *Primal Dream and Primal Crime: Orwell's Development as a Psychological Novelist*. Columbia: University of Missouri Press, 1979.

Peter Stansky and William Abrahams, *Orwell: The Transformation*. New York: Knopf, 1980.

——, *The Unknown Orwell.* New York: Knopf, 1972.

John Thompson, *Orwell's London.* New York: Schocken, 1984.

Richard J. Voorhees, *The Paradox of George Orwell.* Purdue: Purdue University Studies, 1961.

Stephen Wadhams, ed., *Remembering Orwell.* New York: Penguin, 1984.

Raymond Williams, *George Orwell.* London: Fontana/Collins, 1971.

Raymond Williams, ed., *George Orwell: A Collection of Critical Essays.* Englewood Cliffs, NJ: Prentice Hall, 1974.

George Woodcock, *The Crystal Spirit: A Study of George Orwell.* Boston: Little, Brown, 1966.

David Wykes, *A Preface to George Orwell.* New York: Longman, 1987.

Alex Zwerdling, *Orwell and the Left.* New Haven, CT: Yale University Press, 1974.

# WORKS BY GEORGE ORWELL

*Down and Out in Paris and London* (1933)
*Burmese Days* (1934)
*A Clergyman's Daughter* (1935)
*Keep the Aspidistra Flying* (1936)
*The Road to Wigan Pier* (1937)
*Homage to Catalonia* (1939)
*Coming Up for Air* (1939)
*Inside the Whale* (1940)
*The Lion and the Unicorn* (1941)
*Animal Farm* (1945)
*Critical Essays* (1946)
*The English People* (1947)
*1984* (1949)

# INDEX